Kenosis
Christian
Self-Emptying
Meditation

Kenosis

Christian Self-Emptying Meditation

by
Tim Langdell

StillCenter Publications
Oxbridge Publishing, Inc.
Pasadena, CA / Oxford, UK

StillCenter Publications
An imprint of Oxbridge Publishing Inc.
Oxford/Pasadena
530 South Lake Avenue, 171
Pasadena, CA 91101
www.oxbridgepublishing.com

Library of Congress Cataloging-in-Publication Data
Langdell, Tim
      Kenosis: Christian Self-Emptying Meditation / Tim Langdell
         pages cm
    ISBN: 0-9990928-8-X (pbk)
    ISBN-13: 978-0-9990928-8-0 (pbk)
    1. Contemplation   2. Meditation   3. Spirituality   I. Title

Library of Congress Control Number: 2020944352

9 8 7 6 5 4 3 2 1

FIRST EDITION

Kenosis

Christian Self-Emptying Meditation

by

Tim Langdell

StillCenter Publications
Oxbridge Publishing, Inc.
Pasadena, CA / Oxford, UK

StillCenter Publications
An imprint of Oxbridge Publishing Inc.
Oxford/Pasadena
530 South Lake Avenue, 171
Pasadena, CA 91101
www.oxbridgepublishing.com

Library of Congress Cataloging-in-Publication Data
Langdell, Tim
      Kenosis: Christian Self-Emptying Meditation / Tim Langdell
          pages cm
    ISBN: 0-9990928-8-X (pbk)
    ISBN-13: 978-0-9990928-8-0 (pbk)
    1. Contemplation   2. Meditation   3. Spirituality   I. Title

Library of Congress Control Number: 2020944352

9 8 7 6 5 4 3 2 1

FIRST EDITION

"[Christ] made himself nothing"

Phil. 2:7

"In solitude, we are least alone."

Lord Byron

Dedicated my daughter,
Reverend Melissa Campbell-Langdell

contents

preface

This little book is in part made up of extracts from the main work I wrote (*Christ Way, Buddha Way: Jesus as Wisdom Teacher and a Zen Perspective on His Teachings*) and from other of my books on meditation. It does, though, also contain some original writing about *kenosis* that did not appear in those other works.

This book is in part intended for those who have not purchased the *Christ/Buddha* book, and who are primarily interested in finding out more about Christian Meditation, and in particular *kenosis* or "Kenotic Meditation." The style of meditation that we believe Christ himself did. The book also hopefully serves another purpose—that of providing a more portable work that one may take to meditation meetings.

Over the past few decades a new style of contemplative practice emerged known as "Centering Prayer." However, as I argue in this book and its sister volume (the *Christ/Buddha* book), it is unlikely that Christ himself practiced Centering Prayer. From what we know of his personal practice from the gospels—and we know a fair amount—his practice was an entirely silent one. This practice I call "Kenotic Meditation," or *kenosis* for short, or "self-emptying." We thus have reason to believe that while Centering

Prayer has solid foundations in Middle Ages Europe, this practice—*kenosis*—has roots in the first century of the common era.

The further reason for this book is what I see as a real need in the West for an even deeper Christian-based spiritual practice, one founded in silence and rooted in what Jesus actually taught, and one that anyone can practice whether they believe in standard Christian dogma. A practice, then, which is hopefully attractive to both the most devote Christian, and to those who may call themselves "spiritual but not religious"—which, according to Pew Research Reports, is the fastest growing "religion" in the United States).

Indeed, not only are the "spiritual but not religious" (also known as the "nones") the fastest growing segment of the U.S. religious/spiritual population, they are the *only* segment that is growing as Catholic and Protestant segments show continued sharp decline. Interestingly, Pew label this group on their graphs "Nothing in particular:"

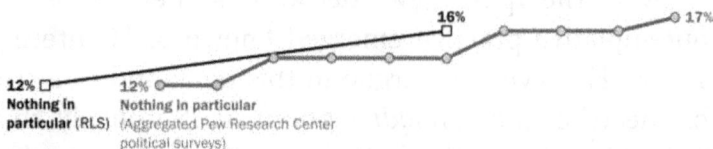

16%   17%
12%   12%
Nothing in   Nothing in particular
particular (RLS)   (Aggregated Pew Research Center
political surveys)

Ironically, *kenosis* is precisely that—self-emptying, which is making yourself nothing—nothing in particular, realizing you are *no-thing*.

4

one

What is Kenosis?

Despite being at the core of Christ's teachings, the terms *kenosis* and "self-emptying" are probably unfamiliar to most Christians. The root of this idea of *kenosis* derives in part from the letter of Paul to the Philippians (2:7) where he says that Christ "emptied himself." And here the word used to translate emptied is a form of the Greek word *keno from which we then get the term kenosis.*

But rather than rely on what Paul said about Christ, we can look at Jesus' own words about his personal spiritual practice:

> [5] *And when you pray, do not be like the hypocrites, for they love to pray standing in the synagogues and on the street corners to be seen by others. Truly I tell you, they have received their reward in full. [6] But when you pray, go into your room, close the door and pray to your Father, who is unseen. Then your Father, who sees what is done in secret, will reward you. [7] And when you pray, do not keep on babbling like pagans, for they think they will be heard because of their many words. [8] Do not be like them, for your Father knows what you*

need before you ask him. Mt (6:5-8)

Thankfully, we also have some idea of Christ's own practice of prayer and meditation:

16 But Jesus often withdrew to lonely places and prayed. (Lk 5:16)

Some translations say that he withdrew into the wilderness to pray (KJV, NASB), and others say he withdrew to deserted places (ISV). In Mark we have further support for this practice of prayer and meditation:

35 Very early in the morning, while it was still dark, Jesus got up, left the house and went off to a solitary place, where he prayed. (Mk 1:35)

And in Mark 6:46: *After leaving them, he went up on a mountainside to pray.*

And in Luke (6:12): *One of those days Jesus went out to a mountainside to pray, and spent the night praying to God.*

And Matthew 14:23: *After he had dismissed them, he went up on a mountainside by himself to pray. Later that night, he was there alone*

What Christ did when he withdrew to these solitary places is not recorded, but we have a clear idea that it was likely silent contemplation, or silent contemplative prayer. Going to this secluded place was not to be alone, since after his awakening he knew there is no such thing as being alone. Alone, after all, is simply the concatenation of the words "all" and "one" (al-one).

He taught others how to pray with what has become to be known as the "Lord's Prayer" (Mt 6:9, Luke 11:2), although this is not present in the older Gospel of Mark. Although the prayer may be familiar to readers, it is worth reading it again as if for the first time.

It starts with "Our Father"—note, not "My Father," but "Our Father." This affirms a repeated theme in Christ's teaching of The Way: namely, that the journey of The Way is from being a child of God (a being in creation, ego-centered, dualistic, the self with a small "s"), to becoming a Son (or Daughter) of God (that is, a state of consciousness where you are aware of your oneness with God, the non-dual state that is characterized by "how may I help you?" and is the Self with a large "S").

One can almost see Christ teaching his followers that they are all children of God and can all become a Son (or Daughter) of God. Possibly some responded, "But aren't you the only son of the Father?" whereupon Christ perhaps rolled his eyes and said, "Once again, God is our Father, not just my Father." Even though this clear statement of absolute equality is enshrined in the prayer he taught, still the drive to pedestalize the man Jesus as a divine figure, standing above and apart from we mere mortals, leads many to overlook the very start of the prayer he taught.

It continues "Our Father *in heaven*" We have learned of course that this 'heaven' of which Christ spoke is not some distant place that one goes to when you die, but rather it is *within you* (Lk 17:21, particularly the King James version[1]). It is a state of consciousness, divine consciousness, that we may all awaken to.

Then in this prayer Christ identified the next key teaching of The Way, namely "Your kingdom come." This was the much misunderstood part of his teaching that evoked for many at the time that Christ was saying he was the Messiah that had been prophesized from time immemorial who would be a leader for the Jews and bring about a new Jewish state. The prophesized Messiah would be a leader of men, a king bringing about an earthly kingdom for the Jews. And remember by this time the Jews had jettisoned kings many years before, and had even jettisoned the priestly class, as well.

This was not what Christ was teaching, He never said he had come to be the prophesized Messiah who would be a leader of men, establishing a new earthly kingdom for the Jews. Rather he was improvising on scripture and re-envisioning the Messianic age as being not a new age for the Jewish peoples, but a new age for all humanity, an age that would be characterized by the emergence of a Kingdom of God, not a kingdom of man. Clarified thus, it becomes readily apparent Christ wasn't saying he was the head of this new kingdom (as the anticipated Messiah would be), but rather it is a kingdom of God with "Our Father" as the King or Lord, not a human like Jesus the Christ.

But as often happened with Christ's teachings, this aspect of what he was saying was misunderstood. It is a pity that there is not a better word for "Kingdom" since it evokes such a masculine concept that echoes for us oppressive regimes by tyrants and despots. Perhaps "Realm" is similar but more neutral. To complicate matters, as was his usual practice Christ was talking in metaphor. Indeed, metaphor on top of metaphor, since he clearly didn't mean a kingdom as such (in the earthly human sense), and he didn't mean king nor did he mean father in the exclusive sense implying men to be superior to women.

What he was referring to by this realm is a state of being in oneness with God, awake to your True Self: non-dual awareness, rather than being stuck in the dualism of "me" and "you," "us" and "them." Just as Zen teaches us that there is nothing to realize, nothing to gain, since we are already awake, already Buddha, just so in Christ's The Way teaching we are all in this Heavenly Realm already: we just have to awaken to that fact.

"*Your Kingdom come,*" then, might better be translated as "*Your Realm is here, now, may it be realized.*" And of course, what follows in the prayer is a very central part of his The Way teaching: *"Your will be done, on earth as it is in heaven."* It is amazing that each day people around the world say these words without stopping to ponder what they mean.

This is the core teaching he repeated over and again: in order to enter the state of consciousness he called heaven within you need to align your will with God's will. To do this you must experience *metanoia*. That is, you need to have a mystical experience, go beyond (*meta*) thought (*noia*). This is the term grossly mistranslated as "repent" in many Bibles as part of an invention of a sin-based theology, quite probably the biggest translation error in the entire New Testament.

To mix the Zen and theistic terms, what he is asking people to pray for is to align the *absolute* (divine) with the *relative* (temporal, human earthly realm of "things"). Achieving this, as he taught, is becoming one with your ground of being, one with God, realizing your Buddha nature. When you do this, your will aligns with God's will. In Zen terms, awaken to your Buddha nature, become fully aware of the absolute and the relative (the 360 point in the prior circle diagram), and right action, right conduct and right speech will naturally follow. Sounds easy doesn't it? But the gate is narrow, remember, and few pass through.

The first four lines of the prayer thus summarize key points of Christ's The Way teachings: the spiritual or theological portion of the prayer, if you will. What

10

follows is the practical portion that deals with the everyday reality of being human. To ask for bread to eat—for basic sustenance—to forgive us as we forgive others, help us not fall into temptation and help us to avoid "evil" ("live" written backwards remember: that is, wrong thought, wrong conduct, wrong action).[2]

There we have it, around 20-30 seconds of word-based prayer. What then? And do we sincerely believe this is what Christ himself prayed when he went alone to those secluded places to pray in secret? Perhaps, but regardless this word-based part of the instruction to prayer is over in a matter of seconds. But in his teachings, accompanying this request to say just one prayer, is an admonishment not to pray like the others do: selfishly asking for things, for personal benefit rather than that of others, and so on. Your Father knows what you want or need better than you, so you don't need to tell him. And most certainly not to do it out loud in public as he noted others doing.

The "Full Cup" Cover Art

You may be wondering why the cover of a book on "self-emptying" features a teacup that is full to over-flowing. There is a reason for it: the idea for the image comes from one of Christ's pithiest sayings:

> *One who has nothing, even what*
> *he has will be taken away.*

This is found in several of Christ's parables, for instance the one about the servants and the talents (Mt 25:14-30).

What does this phrase mean? Some insight into the first century Jewish meaning behind this phrase may be gained from considering Talmud writings. As K.J. Went has observed, the following is a well-known Talmudic writing:

> A mortal can put something into an empty vessel but not into a full one, but the Holy One, blessed be He, is not so, He puts more into a full vessel but not into an empty one. (Babylonian Talmud, *Berakôth*, 40a; *Sukkah* 46a)[3]

There is a famous story that comes to mind based on an Asian source:

> An old sage had a visit from a university professor who came to inquire about The Way. The sage served tea. He poured his visitor's cup full, and then kept on pouring. The professor watched the overflow until he no longer could restrain himself. "It is overfull. No more will go in!" "Like this cup," The old sage said, "you are full of your own opinions and speculations. How can I show you The Way unless you first empty your cup?"[4]

Here are two different cultures and traditions, two almost opposite metaphorical images. In one we have the image of God giving most to someone whose cup is already overflowing, and in the other an old sage who cannot teach someone who is already too full of ideas, concepts and preconceptions.

The Jewish way of thinking, though, gives rise to what some have dubbed the "Matthew effect" (otherwise known as the Matthew principle or the "Matthew effect of accumulated advantage"). Stated simply, the effect says that the rich get richer and the poor get poorer. To those who perform well more tasks and merit are given, to those who underperform, fewer new tasks or rewards are given.

The "Matthew effect" was coined by Robert K. Merton to describe, for instance, how famous researchers get more credit for their work than unknown researchers who do essentially the same work.[5] Seen simplistically, this appears to be what Christ was teaching: if you work actively towards building the Kingdom of God on earth, then God will favor you and reward you, whereas if you are lazy or simply refuse to work toward the Kingdom, then you will fall into God's disfavor and not be rewarded in life.

But the teaching is deeper than that and is ultimately a teaching about dualism versus non-dualism. It is both the joy and the challenge of Christ's parables and sayings that more often than not they can be read on at least two different levels. Here, with these several related parables that contain this phrase, is no exception. At the surface level of understanding, the teachings say that if you work towards establishing the Kingdom of Heaven (on earth) then God will reward you. The harder you work, the more "full" you are of such work, the more you will be rewarded. There is some similarity to a more simplistic view of what they call in the East "karma:" if you do good then good will happen to you. The more good you do the more you benefit. However, this is a simplistic view of karma, not an accurate one.

But the deeper teaching goes to Christ's message about dualistic versus non-dualistic thinking and action. Throughout so many of his parables and sayings, Christ keeps coming back to common themes: develop "don't know" mind, the mind of wonder of a child (child*like* not child*ish*), align your will with God's will (that is, realize your true self, your Christ nature, your oneness with the ground of being), reject attachment to material things, and so on.

While the two approaches (Asian and Jewish wisdom) may at first seem to be at odds—one teaching your cup must be empty, the other that it must be full—they are in fact both addressing essentially the same teaching. Insight into how this can be is gained from appreciating that a core part of Christ's teaching was the practice of *kenosis*, or "self-emptying."

Another way to think of this is that this *kenosis* is an overcoming of ego-based behavior and thought, a transformation from dualistic (ego-based) being to non-dualistic being. An emptying yourself of your "self" (with a small s) and filling yourself with your True "Self" (with a large S). The simple truth is that as you enter into non-dual consciousness then your entire being simultaneously becomes totally empty (of self, ego, dualism), and yet by the very fact of being thus 'empty' is therefore totally full. Non-dual consciousness cannot be partial—it is full to overflowing at all times since it is, after all, awakening.

To evoke a modern parable, it is like the woman who went around with extremely dark glasses on, glasses that turned her world dark and monochromatic, along with blinkers that cut out most of her field of vision. And then one sunny mid-summer day, the woman took off her glasses and removed the blinkers. In that moment she goes from being full of a dark, limited view of the world to be filled with light, color, expanse of vision.

The spiritual transformation from ego-based, dualistic being to non-dualistic fully awakened being is like this. But it isn't the end of the journey: there is then the integration of the dual and the non-dual. To draw the parallel of a compass, realizing non-dual consciousness is like getting to 180—but our journey doesn't end until we get all the way back round to 360, having fully integrated the dual and non-dual (or in alternate terms, the "absolute" and the "relative).

Let's look again at the core teaching Christ is reported to have used in more than one parable: *"as for the one who has nothing, even what he has will be taken away."* (Mt 13:12)

In teaching my students as we work on puzzle-like stories in the Zen tradition (rather like parables in a way—we call them *koans*) I caution them to look out for "the hook." Many have at least one hook, and often there is a core hook. What form this hook takes varies story to story, but in general it is the part of the text that is designed to draw the intellect in. In other cases, it may be just a red herring or a deliberately misleading, or even downright false, statement. But the intellect is drawn to it as if a moth to a flame.

Here in what Christ taught I would suggest the hook is the word "has." Elsewhere in his parables and sayings, Christ focuses on a core part of following "The Way" is to not be attached to material possessions. He speaks of becoming like little children in order to enter the Kingdom of Heaven (within), and of how it is harder for a rich man to achieve this state of consciousness than it is for a camel to pass through the eye of a needle. And elsewhere still he teaches his followers to look at whose face is on a coin: *"Give to Caesar things that are Caesar's and give to God that which is God's."* (Mt 22:21)

These are all part of Christ's core teaching on attachment. The teaching goes like this: so long as you think there is a "you" (or "I") that can "have" things, you will not be able to realize your Christ nature. To believe you "have" things is central to dualist thinking, and a core illusion that keeps us from being awake to

16

who we truly are.

Thus, perhaps credit to the writer of Luke who added in the nuance of "even what he thinks he has will be taken from him" (Lk 8:18). It's a transformative road we travel that goes from "Oh woe is me, I have nothing" to "How amazing, I have nothing!" As paradoxical as it may seem, it is not until we fully realize our true nature is not to "have things" that we can become empty and thereby have everything. But here the "have" is synonymous with "being:" we realize our oneness with everything (non-dual awareness) means that we are everything. There is no "me" and (separate from) "it," "me" and (separate from) "you."

Yet as I have said before, this realization gets us to 180: when we get there we still have to integrate the reality of being human—of what is meant by form rather than formlessness—and ultimately the realization at 360 that we are both separate and not separate. That the relative and the absolute are not two different "things" or concepts: God (absolute) and God's creation (relative) are not two separate "things."

In Christ's teaching, we are both human and divine: we are one with God (a Son or Daughter of God) and thus with the entire universe, but there is still a real sense in which we are individual human beings (children of God). We are God pretending to be human, pretending to be God. And with that, we touch on the whole idea of incarnation which is addressed elsewhere in this book. In us, God plays hide and seek

17

with God.

A central theme of many parables and sayings by Christ is *kenosis*: the emptying of the self. Only by emptying ourselves (of the ego, or dualistic thinking), he taught, can we become full of God. Elsewhere Christ refers to this as setting aside our will and aligning ourselves with God's will. This, he teaches, makes one who achieves such alignment a Son (or Daughter) of God. And he contrasts this idea of becoming a "Son of God" with being a child of God—part of God's creation, a unique individual in a universe of unique individuals.

Thus, in Christ's teaching to be a "Son of God" (or Daughter) is the non-dualistic state of being, in contrast to identifying as a "child of God," which is the dualistic state of being. Sadly, this essential, powerful, teaching by Christ gets hidden in the traditional teachings of the established Christian Church. From shortly after his death, it seems there was an immediate push to reinvent Jesus as something "other" and unattainable, a divine being dwelling temporarily in a human body.

From shortly after Jesus' death, starting perhaps with the teachings of Saul of Tarsus (later known as "St. Paul"), writers hurriedly tried to rewrite history in order to elevate—or *pedestalize*—Jesus as a kind of magical being. Hence, only Jesus could be "the" Christ, and only Jesus could be "the" (only) Son of God. By the time the Gospel of John was written, one or two lifetimes after Jesus' death, the audience for such writings had solidly become those who were being taught to believe that Christ was someone *other*, someone beyond a mere mortal, who was and had achieved things that no one else could ever achieve. This was not, however, what Jesus taught during his lifetime.

During his lifetime we have a fairly clear record from the synoptic Gospels (Matthew, Mark and Luke) that whenever any of Christ's followers tried to put Christ on a pedestal and say he was the only Son of God, the chosen one, the Messiah, an other-worldly divine being, he replied, "Who do you say I am?" In these early Gospels Christ does not claim to be *the* Son of God or *the* Messiah. This message is clouded, however, by later additions and changes to all three Gospels adding in text well after his death to the effect that Christ admitted he was the Messiah and swore his followers to secrecy that he had admitted this fact (from which follows, if they were sworn to secrecy how could the writer know this? He couldn't, of course).

Here is another useful observation: note how many times in the Gospels—especially Mark and Matthew, the earliest ones—that it is said that something happened in secret or that Christ asked those present not to speak of what was said. This is usually a clue to wording that has been added later to support the post-crucifixion narrative that sought to pedestalize Jesus. Have you ever stopped to ask yourself, in these passages where Jesus is meant to have ordered those present not to say anything, how did it come to be written down? Or if the text indicates something happened in secret, or without a witness, how did that come to be written down?

You can, of course, dismiss such an observation by saying "well, despite his order to say nothing someone must have said something." But this is not likely. Although tradition has the four Gospels named after disciples, there is wide agreement that none of them were written by any of Christ's followers. Nor do we believe that any of Christ's disciples contributed directly to the writing of any of the Gospels. The earliest Gospel writings seem to date from around 66 C.E., or at least 33 years after the crucifixion.

By this point you will have presumably worked out why the image of an overflowing cup was chosen for the cover, and for a repeated motif in this book. It represents who we are as we start on this path of The Way—the full cup, and the need to empty ourselves.

---

[1] *"Neither shall they say, Lo here! or, lo there! for, behold, the kingdom of God is within you."* (Luke 17:21, KSV)

[2] It is arguable it is all spiritual since "bread" could also refer to Christ's teaching, and atonement together with forgiveness are key parts of a spiritual practice. Christ clearly played with the symbolism of bread as manna from heaven, here for him in the form of teachings, the word of God: "Man shall not live on bread alone, but on every word that comes from the mouth of God." Mt. 4:4

[3] https://www.studylight.org/language-studies/difficult-sayings.html

[4] Paul Reps, *Zen Flesh, Zen Bones,* Tuttle, 1957

[5] Merton, Robert K. (1968). *The Matthew Effect in Science.* Science, 159 (3810): 56–63.

two

Contemplation: A Brief History of Silent Prayer

We need to review the scripture well known to Christ and his followers to more fully appreciate the context here of the instruction to pray in secret and to not speak out loud. Praying out loud was common in the ancient world, and indeed was clearly still common in Christ's day, too. But it would have been well known to at least his Jewish followers that there is a famous reference in the Hebrew Bible (Old Testament) to silent prayer:

> [12] *As she kept on praying to the LORD, Eli observed her mouth.* [13] *Hannah was praying in her heart, and her lips were moving but her voice was not heard. Eli thought she was drunk* (1 Sam 1:12-13)

This would be an appropriate moment to clarify that what Eastern traditions call meditation tends to be known as contemplation in the Christian tradition, and vice versa. Thus, while meditation is usually thought of in Eastern traditions as the act of sitting silently, in Christianity it has been more usual to term this (silent) contemplation. By contrast, Christians have tended to talk of meditation as something that is done on a subject or topic: hence, we talk of meditating *on* a passage from the Bible or meditating *on* love.

That clarified, there were at least four key forces influencing Christ's view of silent prayer and contemplation: the Jewish tradition that included Hannah's prayer; Christ's obvious awareness of Mahayana Buddhist traditions and practice (as shown by his use of Buddhist parables); Christ's familiarity through John the Baptist and others of the first century Gnostic, Essene and other ascetic practices; and, finally, the ever pervasive presence of Hellenist thought including the fledgling beginnings of what would come to be known as Neoplatonism.

Of course, as we have seen earlier, these are not distinct influences but rather interconnected ways of thought and practice which each probably influenced the other. Gnosticism arose in the first century C.E. as Christianity was being birthed and as Mahayana Buddhism was spreading throughout the Middle East. Some have suggested the Gnosticism has its roots partly in Buddhism and perhaps Hinduism, others argue for the influence of Platonism.[1] Certainly, the Gnostic emphasis on illusion and enlightenment evokes parallels with both Buddhism and Platonism (and as we have discussed, it is probable that Platonism, and particularly Neoplatonism, itself was influenced by Buddhism). A high degree of syncretism is very likely during this period.

The Essenes are perhaps an even more likely influence on Christ since much of what they espoused closely matches Christ's teachings. We have some historic knowledge of the Essenes and know they grew in popularity from around a hundred years or so before Christ on in to the first century C.E. Once again, their emergence roughly tracks the emergence of Mahayana Buddhism in this same period.

Jospehus, the Jewish historian, writes that the Essenes flourished in Roman Judea at the time of Christ, certainly numbering in the thousands while not as numerous as either the Sadducees or the Pharisees. Pliny the Elder first recorded details of the Essenes, reporting that they lived simply in communities, that their leaders were known as contemplatives, favored having no money or possessions, ritually immersed themselves in water each morning, and emphasized benevolence and charity.[2]

Indeed, Bratton[3] notes that one early leader of the Essenes ("The Teacher of Righteousness") sounds a lot like Christ:

> *The Teacher of Righteousness of the Scrolls would seem to be a prototype of Jesus, for both spoke of the New Covenant; they preached a similar Gospel; each was regarded as a Savior or Redeemer; and each was condemned and put to death by reactionary factions ...We do not know whether Jesus was an Essene, but some scholars feel that he was at least influenced by them.*

Of course, it would be natural to ask the question whether John the Baptist was an Essene. Afterall, like the Essenes he emphasized baptism and asceticism. We cannot know with any certainty, but it seems likely he was not since Essenes appear to have kept themselves separate from general society and would not have been out and about preaching as we are told John was. Moreover, records report that the Essenes favored wearing simple white robes to reflect purity, rather than the rough camel's hair closing and leather belt we are told John wore.

That said, it is entirely possible that John was influenced by the Essenes and borrowed some of their basic practices (notably immersion in water) and teachings to spread as a lone hermit rather than as part of an established community.

What all these first century Jewish groups had in common, though, aside from asceticism and eschewing personal possessions, was a focus on contemplation, silence and a spiritual practice that involved withdrawal from society to contemplate. Surprisingly, little detail exists in the texts of precisely what these groups practiced but we can triangulate their approach to prayer from what we do know. They were referred to as "contemplatives," they emphasized hermit like living and solitary practice, and nowhere is it written that they prayed out loud to themselves (as if chanting, or etc.).

From all this we can conclude with some reasonable certainty that there was a general focus on silent prayer or contemplation in these communities and the practices they encouraged in their members. Such contemplative practices were also associated with Platonists and the Hellenistic Stoics. Both these Greek groups spoke of a God within that one should commune with. And as Pieter W van der Horst wrote in his article titled *Silent Prayer in Antiquity*:[4]

Communing with a God who is within you can be accomplished without words, say the Stoics.

What is also compelling is that practices that had their beginnings around the time of Christ went on to specifically teach the practice of silent prayer and contemplation. Particularly, for instance, the emerging practice of *via negativa* which had its roots in ascetic practices and was later characterized by such seminal works as the fourteenth century *The Cloud of Unknowing*. Evelyn Underhill tells us that *The Cloud* was based on the mystical writings of Pseudo-Dionysius the Areopagite specifically and on Christian Neoplatonism generally.

Pseudo-Dionysius was an anonymous Christian philosopher active around late 600 to early 700 C.E. known for a set of works, the *Corpus Dionysiacum*. He took his name from the Athenian convert of Paul mentioned in Acts 17:34—hence the term "pseudo" since he was not alleging the author of the works was that actual person mentioned in Acts. The basic ideas espoused in *The Cloud* can also be traced back to the *Confessions of St. Augustine* written between 397 and 400 C.E.

Thus, while we cannot join all of the dots exactly for a tradition of silent prayer and contemplation from the time before Christ through to his teachings, we can trace a solid history of the practice in the Middle East from ancient Jewish tradition, through the practices of first century ascetics, on to the later traditions of silent prayer and contemplation in the various Christian monastic traditions. These contemplative traditions culminate in modern Centering Prayer[5] and the revitalization in this book and elsewhere of kenotic practice[6] as the confluence of the silent prayer taught in *The Cloud of Unknowing* and Zen.

The *via negativa*, also known as apophatic theology, is often associated with mysticism and mystical experience. It is a way that realizes that ultimate truth cannot be described in words. Hence, this approach is associated with reports of experiences of oneness with God, or oneness with everything (to use non-theological language) rather than intellectual description or speculation about the nature of God or oneness with God. The use of words, and in particular the converse *kataphatic* theology (or *cataphatic*, "positive way"), seeks to describe the ultimate reality using positive attributes such as "God is love," or "God is good."

In the writings of Pseudo Dionysius he emphasized

the importance of both ways of approaching understanding or appreciation of the divine. He saw the *kataphatic* approach as an affirmative way of understanding transcendence using positive attributes, and the apophatic way as stressing God's absolute transcendence and unknowability. Why this is of interest to us here is that what he wrote has parallels to Zen: just as he wrote that it is ultimately important to 'understand' God as both *imminent* (known, named) and *transcendent* (unknowable), in Zen we have the parallel of the *relative* (the named; dualism) and the *absolute* (beyond naming or before thought; non-dualism).

Closely aligned with *via negativa* as a parallel 'way' to approach the ultimate is *agnosticism*. In modern parlance, agnosticism may invoke the idea of 'atheist-lite' or even 'believer-lite.' Indeed, many even confuse agnosticism with atheism, merging both into the category of 'nonbeliever.' Agnosticism conjures up the image of someone who is not quite sure about God: "Maybe I believe in God, maybe I don't. I not sure." But that isn't technically what agnosticism means and did not mean that when the discipline or movement started millennia ago.

Strictly speaking, agnosticism is the view that God, the ground of being, or the ultimate nature of reality (whatever term works best for you), is essentially unknowable. Hence the agnostic seeker in the first century use of the term has much in common with the apophatic seeker who also considers God or the ultimate reality to be unknowable and not capable of being described in words. This has a direct parallel in Zen to what we refer to as "don't know mind," or "beginners mind"—the state of being before thought (or beyond thought; we are back again to Jesus' *metanoia*).

These practices, or 'ways,' of *via negativa* and *agnosis* were not rare or fringe views, on the contrary some of the better known theologians, monks, sages, saints, and mystics of the past two thousand years have followed one of these paths. And of course, they formed the basis of both the works of Pseudo Dionysius and the author of the fourteenth century classic text *The Cloud of Unknowing*.

While the basic ideas behind apophatic thought substantially predate the time of Christ, what is of particular interest is that some scholars such as Carabine[7] argue that as a practice it really got going with Philo of Alexandria who lived from around 20 B.C.E. to about 50 C.E. He was a Hellenistic Jewish philosopher who was based in Alexandria which at that time was in the Roman province of Egypt.

Why this is especially interesting is that this is also precisely when Buddhism was flourishing in Alexandria, and of course apophatic views, like the emergence of Mahayana Buddhism, overlapped exactly with the life of Christ. Moreover, both of these movements—the growing Mahayana Buddhist movement and the apophatic one—were spreading throughout Palestine at the exact time Christ was absorbing every religious way and philosophy he could as he sought revelation and thereafter prepared to teach.[8]

This is doubly important since Philo is known for synthesizing Jewish scripture with Greek Stoic philosophy, and it was his ideas that brought forth ideas like the *Logos* as an aspect of God which of course found its way into the Gospel of John. While some dispute it, Philo seems to have had a sizable influence over early Christianity as his concept of the demiurge of the world, next only to God himself, is the *Logos*, God's shadow, God's firstborn son. The writer of John drew heavily on such concepts.

But such ideas can be a distraction from a more important point: namely that Philo was integrating Jewish scripture with stoicism. For many, stoicism brings to mind an ethical system encouraging someone to live a good life free of moral corruption. But what is less often emphasized is that Stoics believed in practicing spiritual exercises including self-dialog, contemplation of one's mortality, and—most important—training the mind to be fully present in the moment. This Stoic contemplation practice, as later described by writers such as Marcus Aurelius, sounds a lot like Buddhist mindfulness meditation.[9]

Thus we have the philosophical thought arising in the Hellenistic world of the nature of the One, starting with Plato, being developed by the likes of Philo, and leading to the seminal works of Proclus[10] in the fifth century where Neoplatonic views start to have greater and greater influence on Early Christianity. But during the time of Christ, there was this emergence of the pre-Neoplatonic era where many of the ideas later developed by Pseudo Dionysius and others had their beginnings.

It is this school of thought espoused by Philo and others, that emphasized the idea of *God within* and of silent meditation to focus the mind on the present moment: focus the mind on being at one with God, meditating in silence. With this view of the divine came the idea that there is The One, and that it is the ultimate goal of a spiritual path to become one with The One.

As Pieter W van der Horst said in his *Silent Prayer in Antiquity*, "*Communing with a God who is within you can be accomplished without words, say the Stoics.*"[11] Thus, while we lack written evidence of the exact practice of prayer and meditation Christ used when he withdrew to one of his solitary places, we do know that he was influenced by Buddhism, the Jewish Wisdom tradition (including the ways of the ascetics) along with the Hellenistic thought of the Stoics and the early stages of what came to be known as Neoplatonism (or, specifically, Christian Neoplatonism). And each of these ways or philosophies urged the use of silent meditation or focusing of the mind on the present moment in order to seek spiritual revelation or oneness.

We have a line we can now draw regarding silent prayer and meditation from the time before Christ with Platonic ideas and the Stoics, through the works of Philo and the emergence in parallel at this time of Mahayana Buddhism in Alexandria (where Philo was also based), through the Jewish Wisdom tradition of the first century, through practices such as Hesychasm, and on through the Neoplatonist tradition in the centuries that followed, on through to the writing of *The Cloud of Unknowing* in the fourteenth century. The ultimate guide to contemplative prayer of medieval times, which merged with Zen forms modern day Centering Prayer practice, and revived kenotic practices such as presented later in this book.

Hesychasm is a contemplative prayer practice established within the Eastern Orthodox Church. The term means to keep stillness and has its roots in the synoptic Gospels where Christ advises going to a room and praying to your Father in secret (Mt 6:6). The origins of the practice date back to the writings of Evangrius Ponticus (349-399 C.E.) and Maximus the Confessor (580-662 C.E.). Others using the term in the early church include St. John Chrysostom and the Cappadocians, and in the *Sayings of the Desert Fathers* (approx. 5th century).

The goal of this form of mystical contemplation is to attain union with God (*Theosis*). The three phases of the practice include *Katharsis* (purification), *Theoria* (illumination) and then finally *Theosis* (union with

31

God). Key to this practice is the use of the Jesus Prayer: *"Lord Jesus Christ, son of God, have mercy on me, a sinner."* Repetition of this phrase is used to move the contemplative through the stages until, at *Theosis,* there is oneness with God that is spoken of in terms of God as light, so-called "uncreated light," which they also identify with the Holy Spirit. Very often, Hesychasts (as practitioners are known) live a life of hermits to devote themselves completely to this mystical path.

The Cloud of Unknowing is a good early source of guidance on how to engage in contemplation. The *Cloud* espouses a mystical approach to Christianity that sees God as beyond knowing and encourages the follower to abandon the ego to a state of consciousness best described as "unknowing." If this route is followed, the author suggests, then one may gain a glimpse of the true nature of God, become one with God.

Clearly, *The Cloud* draws heavily on the *via negativa* school, and has much in common with the earlier apophatic tradition that came about in the time of Christ. Here then is a tradition from the fourteenth century that has its roots in the writings of St, Augustine and Pseudo Dionysius, and which influenced the likes of St John of the Cross, Nicholas of Cusa and Teilhard de Chardin.

We don't know who wrote *The Cloud* and it seems fitting that it drew in large part from the works of

Pseudo Dionysius who also remained anonymous. It is open to speculation, but perhaps in both cases the writers feared retribution for writing what some might call heretical works. *The Cloud* encourages abandoning thought in order to reach a state of unknowing in which one may commune with the divine. This *cloud of unknowing* as the writer calls it is referred to as a darkness that is between you and God stopping you from seeing the divine clearly and directly.

The work recommends focusing on a single word as a way to entering into stillness and full contemplation:

> *We must pray, then, with all the intensity of our being in its height and depth and length and breadth. And not with many words but in a little word of one syllable.*[12]

He goes on to clarify which words he recommends be used and settles on "God" and "sin." He elaborates that no two other words so succinctly sum up the totality of being, the essentially good and the essentially bad. Moreover, he advises that having chosen a word you should repeat it with "intensity" which evokes a kind of mantra practice where a phrase of word is repeated over and again. However, he makes clear that this repetition is of a contemplative nature, not the fast-paced repetition often used in Hindu or Muslim chanting.

Elsewhere the author of *The Cloud* says:

> *Contemplatives rarely pray in words, but if they
> do, their words are few. The fewer the better, as a
> matter of fact; yes, a word of one syllable is more
> suited to the spiritual nature of this work than
> longer ones.* (95)

And here he likens sin to being a 'lump' and
describes the demeanor of one who is in
contemplation as seeming completely relaxed and
peaceful:

> *For I believe that a dark generalized awareness
> of sin (intending only yourself but in an
> undefined way, like a lump) should incite you to
> the fury of a caged wild animal. Anyone looking
> at you, however, would not notice any change in
> your expression, and suppose that you are quite
> calm and composed. Sitting, walking, lying down,
> resting, standing, or kneeling, you would appear
> completely relaxed and peaceful.* (94-95)

The writer also commends moderation and
adopting contemplation as central to a way of life:

> *That by having no moderation in
> contemplation a man will arrive at perfect
> moderation in everything else."* (p 101, header to
> chapter 42) *"That a man must lose the radical
> self-centered awareness of his own being if he will
> reach the heights of contemplation in this life.*
> (102, header to chapter 43)

Then continuing in chapter 43 he introduces what he calls the *cloud of forgetting*:

> *Be careful to empty your mind and heart of everything except God during the time of this work. Reject the knowledge and experience of anything less than God, treading it all down beneath the cloud of forgetting."* ... *"And now also you must learn to forget not only every creature and its deeds but yourself as well, along with whatever you may have accomplished in God's service. For a true lover not only cherishes his beloved more than himself but in a certain sense he becomes oblivious of himself on account of the one he loves.*

And then he introduces the idea of "naked knowing" and the goal of destroying the self (ego) as being a state of pure love:

> *Long after you have successful forgotten every creature and its works, you will find that a naked knowing and feeling of your own being still remains between you and your God. And believe me, you will not be perfect in love until this, too, is destroyed.*

And then chapter 44 he gives a description of how the self (ego) is to be 'destroyed' by freedom from knowing, but without self (bodily) harm:

> *And yet, in all this, never does he desire to not-*

be, for this is the devil's madness and blasphemy against Got. In fact, he rejoices that he is and from the fullness of a grateful heart he gives thanks to God for the gift and the goodness of his existence. At the same time, however, he desires unceasingly to be freed from the knowing and the feeling of his being.

Two other notable authors we should consider are Meister Eckhart and more recently still the writings of Angelus Silesius. Meister Eckhart was a Catholic German mystic and theologian who lived from 1260-1328 C.E. His writings are truly remarkable, and I heartily recommend that you explore them. Importantly, what he wrote speaks to this topic of discovering God within, and the importance of stillness, quiet and contemplation as the path to God within.

Perusing quotes from his works shows how pertinent he is to our discussion here: "*A quiet mind is one which nothing weighs on, nothing worries, which, free from ties and from all self-seeking, is wholly merged into the will of God and dead to its own [will].*"

And a further selection:

Unmovable disinterest brings man into likeness of God ... To be full of things is to be empty of God, to be empty of things is to be full of God."
"*All that the Eternal Father teaches and reveals is His being, His nature, and His Godhead, which*

he manifests to us in His Son, and teaches us
that we are also His Son.

Not surprisingly, then, Eckhart favored silent contemplation as a way to seek unity with God. And as you can see, like Christ he emphasized the need to align one's will with God's will, a said that we are [God's] Son just as Christ is. A revolutionary theological position to take in the middle ages. A similar writer worthy of exploration on this topic is Angelus Silesius. He also was a Catholic mystic, and lived from 1624-1677 C.E. Here is a sampling of his poetry:

True prayer requires no word, no chant
no gesture, no sound.
It is communion, calm and still
with our own Godly Ground

God far exceeds all words that we can here express
In silence He is heard, in silence worshiped best

Even before I was me, I was God in God;
And I can be once again, as soon as I am dead to
myself

Time is eternity and eternity is time, just as long as
you yourself don't make them different

Two eyes our souls possess:
While one is turned on time,
The other seeth things

This we find the line extending from centuries before Christ, through the middle ages to the Renaissance and beyond, with a repeated focus on the importance of silence in the pursuit of unity with God, and constant theme of self-emptying. Continuing this line through to the present day, we have the work of Father Thomas Keating and the advent of Centering Prayer, and through this and various other works, the revived practice of Kenotic Contemplation.

Centering Prayer has its roots in the work of Thomas Keating when he was the abbot of St. Joseph's Abbey in Spencer, Massachusetts from 1961-1981. During the latter period of his time as abbot he and his fellow monks invited a Zen master to introduce them to the idea of a "sesshin" (week-long intensive retreat) and from this, coupled with reviving the ideas in *The Cloud of Unknowing*, Buddhist Zen meditation became Centering Prayer. We will explore this all further in the next chapter.

While we shall explore it in more depth in the next chapter, it is tempting to liken the kind of meditation that Christ himself practiced to Zazen. While we can never know precisely how he practiced, as we have discussed he favored retreating to a secluded place and sitting in silence. His repeated invitation to align your will with God's will, and the need to achieve *metanoia* in order to enter heaven within, and his general admonition of praying out loud, is all suggestive of a silent form of prayerful meditation. In the next chapter we shall explore this and tease out the difference between Centering Prayer and Kenotic Meditation as practices to follow in replicating Christ's "The Way."

[1] For instance, see Pagels, Elaine (1989). *The Gnostic Gospels* New York: Random House.

[2] Pliny the Elder. *Historia Naturalis.* V 17 or 29.

[3] Bratton, Fred Gladstone (1967). *A History of the Bible.* Boston: Beacon Press, 79-80

[4] Pieter W van der Horst. *Silent Prayer in Antiquity* in the journal *Numen*, Vol 41 No 1 Jan 1994, pp 1-25.

[5] Keating, Thomas (1994). *Intimacy with God* New York: Crossroads Publishing

[6] See the final chapter of this book.

[7] Carabine, Deidre (2015), *The Unknown God: Negative Theology in the Platonic Tradition*, Eugene Oregon: Wipf and Stock Publishers

[8] If you'd like to read more about the presence of Buddhism in the Middle East at the time of Christ, I recommend my sister book, *Christ Way, Buddha Way: Jesus as Wisdom Teacher and a Zen Perspective on His Teachings*, StillCenter Publications, 2020.

[9] *Meditations*, a series of writings by Marcus Aurelius, a Roman Emperor from 161 to 180 C.E.

[10] Carobine, *ibid.*

[11] Horst, *ibid.*

[12] Johnston, William (Ed.) *The Cloud of Unknowing* (1973) New York: Doubleday. Ch 37, 97.

three

Christ's "The Way"

According to the historical record we have of Jesus and his followers, those who followed his teachings referred to themselves as followers of "The Way."[1] Indeed, in the Gospel of John the writer has Jesus describing himself as *the way, the truth and the life*[2] and the synoptic Gospels mention "The Way" at least eight times.[3] This raises the question, why were Christ's followers known as those following "The Way" and what was this "Way?"

Other than Christ's teachings, Zen is the other spiritual path that is also known as "The Way," or "The Buddha Way." While it was many generations later, the famous Zen master Dogen was using this terminology in such a way that it appeared to have been in use for centuries.

> *To study the Buddha Way is to study the self. To study the self is to forget the self. To forget the self is to be actualized by myriad things. When actualized by myriad things, your body and mind as well as the bodies and minds of others drop away. No trace of enlightenment remains, and this no-trace continues endlessly.*[4]

Could Jesus have got the idea of calling his teachings "The Way" from visiting Buddhists?

While we know nothing about most of Christ's adult life before he started teaching at around the age of 30, it seems very likely that he would have been exploring a wide range of religious and spiritual teachings as he explored his own personal spiritual path and calling. Whether Christ himself ever came into contact with any Buddhists, it seems likely he did: he was immersed in the spiritual trends of his time including the teachings of the Essences, Gnostics, etc., any of whom may themselves have absorbed some of the new Buddhist Mahayana way. Major philosophical thinkers and teachers based in Alexandria, including Buddhists who had settled there from the East or Greeks who had become Buddhists, significantly influenced the region.

The similarities between Mahayana teachings and those of the Gnostics at the time of Christ have been well documented elsewhere by writers like Marcus Borg and Elaine Pagels,[5] so we know there were many sects that had Eastern influences around that time. After his encounter with John the Baptist, Christ then retreats to the desert to fast and prayer in silence for forty days and forty nights. The parallels between Christ and Buddha are striking at times: not only does Jesus go on an extended forty-day retreat at about age thirty, but Buddha reputedly similarly sits quietly for forty days at age thirty-five.[6]

Was this when Christ encountered desert communities with spiritual teachers who had become familiar with Buddhist ways of thought and the term "The Way?" Or did religious thought arising in the Middle East around the last century B.C.E. and first century C.E. find its way back along the Silk Road to India and China to influence the rise of Mahayana Buddhism? We may never know but most important, aside from noting key similarities and parallels, we should not get hung up on this. Again, our key concern here is not historical, factual "truth" but a more fundamental and universal "Truth"—what you find true for you. Ultimately, what you find useful on your spiritual journey or in your meditation, contemplation or centering prayer practice.

Although somewhat of a simplification, in both India at the time of Buddha and in the Middle East at the time of Christ, established religions tended to speak to the rules someone should follow. Religion tended to tell someone what to eat, what to recite, when to recite it, what to believe, what not to believe, and so on. Both Buddha and Christ, by contrast, introduced this alternate option of having a path—a Way—to an ultimate realization or goal, and followers were invited to join this path and travel it with a teacher.

A key part of Christ's "The Way" is silent contemplation: what we call *kenosis* or Kenotic Meditation.

---

[1] Acts 9:2, 18:24-26, 19:9, 19:23, 24:14, 24:22
[2] Jn 14:16

3 Mt. 7:13, 7:14, 22:16, Mark 1:3, 12:14, Luke 1:79, 3:4, 20:21

4 *Shobogenzo* by Eihei Dogen

5 Marcus Borg, *Meeting Jesus Again for the First Time: The Historical Jesus and the Heart of Contemporary Faith*. HarperOne, 1995.

Elaine Pagels, *The Gnostic Gospels*, Random House, 1981

6 There is a longer summary of the parallels between the life of Christ and the life of the Buddha in Appendix 2.

four

Why Meditate? Why Follow The Way?

The Dalai Lama has said that the main purpose of life is happiness. Many of us, though, would settle for a day with less stress in it than the prior day. The idea of being happy all the time may sound attractive, but few human beings see that as possible in their day to day lives. Indeed, a perpetual state of happiness—in the sense we usually mean that—invokes some kind of 1960s hippie concept. Walking around with a perpetual smile no matter how awful what is happening in the world may be isn't a balanced, healthy state to be in.

Indeed, The Way does not teach that our goal is to be happy, rather if this is a time for sadness (at, say the loss of a loved one), then be 100% sad. Enter fully into that sadness. If you have reason to be happy, then, sure, be 100% happy. Enter fully into that. The Way is about waking up to exactly who you are, which carries with it a full embodiment of all your emotions. But for most human beings controlling their emotions, or indeed fully embodying them, is not even on the radar as a key goal in life.

Rather, particularly in the West, we are very self-centered and see progress or success as measured by

45

how much more one has achieved today than yesterday. We come from a position of seeing ourselves as less than perfect, less than what we could be, and reject our ability to have self-awareness—which is sad since it is one of our greatest gifts. Instead, we focus on "improving" ourselves or our situation. But what if I told you that you are perfect just as you are (although you could use some improvement, as master teacher Shunryu Suzuki said)? You would probably call me mad.

We're forever looking outside of ourselves for solutions that will make us feel better, feel more perfect. If only we had a better job, if only we had more money, if only we knew the right people. If we look to ourselves at all, then it is for some societal based goal such as, "If only I could be slimmer," or, "If only my muscles were more toned." Yes, we may have worthy goals such as seeking to be healthier, but rarely is seeking health seen as a main human goal. We always want more.

Yet, the fact you are reading this book probably means you sense something deeper: you perhaps sense that beyond all these petty human selfish goals or greater wealth and social standing is a more important truth: that you are deep down limitless and boundless. That there is no limit to your potential, but something is persistently getting in the way of you seeing how to realize this deeper truth.

For many of us realization starts to dawn as we get older, for some it can come earlier in life. We have switched jobs and found we are still lacking something. The job seemed to be what was holding us back from achieving our true goal, but no matter how many job changes it always seems unsatisfying. Or perhaps you are lucky enough to have a major promotion with a sizable increase in salary, yet still you don't feel satisfied. With greater income comes society's pressure to want more, almost as if no matter how much you earn it would never be sufficient. Indeed, if you are looking for this deeper sense of achieving a core life goal, it will never come from these external achievements. And perhaps that has dawned on you by this point, hence you are exploring The Way.

You have maybe run down your many lists of "If only I could ..." and come to the conclusion that none of these goals actually left you feeling more satisfied, more whole. Of course, if you're not careful, The Way can bring a whole new list of "If only" possibilities. If only I could work out what oneness with God really is. If only I could do my Way lessons. If only I could wear fancy robes. If only I could become a fully certified follower of The Way—the temptation to find what you are looking for out there in titles and so-called achievements has the potential to dog you in The Way as it has dogged you in the rest of your life.

Although it can be very hard to appreciate, the problems you perceive arise mainly from your belief that you are a person in a world full of entirely separate, independent other people. You are essentially a thing, an object, defined by various societal labels and norms. When you meet strangers in a social gathering, it's likely initial questions involve ones such as "What do you do for a living?" or "What part of town do you live in?" or "Have you lived here long?" or "How do you know the host of this event?"

Inherent in such questions are concepts that define you in relation to these labels and definitions that society—other people—have decided are what define you. Thus, in response to your saying what you do for a living, the other person may privately think, or even say out loud, "Oh that, I could never live on the wage that job gives." Or, "Oh that part of town, isn't it rather dangerous?" Or perhaps, "Oh you know a friend of the host, well I know the host himself." Even when there is a sincere attempt not to judge and compare, still judgment and comparison happens daily in many of our social interactions. And they subtly help form your view of "who you are" as defined by all these external measures.

What is central to all this of course is the idea that you are a separate individual, limited, struggling to be a better individual, to be more successful as an individual. But this also means that whether you feel good, whether you suffer, whether you are lifted up or put down, is all in the hands of others "out there." The ways this mode of thinking can corrupt us are endless. It can lead to a way of thinking that is driven by "What is in it for me?" rather than "How will this benefit others?"

So, we get a better job so that *we* benefit, not others. So that *we* get more money, not others. To this part of you may be thinking, "Well, of course! Why wouldn't I want to benefit from what I achieve in life?" But that is the narrow view we all get sucked into: the view of ourselves as an object that can become a better object. And that all we need to be concerned with is how *this* object (person) is doing, no regard for others since whether they fail or succeed is entirely up to them. What we fail to see is this mode of thinking is *precisely* our main problem. It is dualistic thinking that can only result in suffering.

We thus turn to a spiritual path to address our need to better ourselves, or to seek a deep personal peace or happiness. Will The Way give that to you? The more familiar you become with The Way, the more you will come to expect answers that are contradictory. These questions—of whether a spiritual path will give you certain results—are examples of what in The Way are called "gaining mind." That is, goals and expectations that you are going to gain something from this practice.

In fact, this practice is about letting everything drop away, rather than gaining anything—self-emptying, *kenosis*. I mentioned earlier that the term "enlightenment" is not well-liked in The Way circles since it implies something you gain. The common phrase is "to become enlightened" which is almost the polar opposite of what The Way practice and teaching is all about. As confounding as it may sound, you are already enlightened you merely have to realize that by becoming fully awake to your true self, your Christ-nature.

Following the path of The Way is not for the faint hearted: it takes dedication and discipline. It turns out that it is surprisingly hard to achieve something that is both fundamentally simple and straightforward, and yet cannot be gained by achievement. Much like learning to ride a bicycle, listening to talks, watching videos, reading books, will only get you so far: to walk this path you will need to devote yourself to it since only you can awaken yourself, no one can awaken you for you.

Thus, whether you choose to pursue *kenosis* as your practice, or work on parables with a teacher, or a mixture of the two, you will need courage to devote yourself fully. This is not a path that you pursue for a few weeks or months and expect a "result." Again, that is gaining mind. The Way calls for a commitment of years, perhaps the entirety of your adult life. The wonderful flipside of this is that the practice becomes your entire life, and it will be a life fully lived in a way that you likely cannot achieve by virtually any other practice.

There will be ups and downs: there will be times when you may feel on top of the world. You find a deep inner peace, and everything feels particularly right with the world. Then, without warning, perhaps things will feel as grey as grey can be, with a sense that you have practiced for years but gotten nowhere (this is technically true, of course, but that doesn't mean it can't be very saddening). It is another The Way conundrum that while what you think of as your "ego" is illusionary, it can be this ego that leads to the highs and lows. Perhaps clearly, perhaps subtly, the feeling that *"I've made it! I'm a spiritual being with all this Zen work! I am one with everything! I get it!"* can creep in and rewards you with a sense of ecstasy. Yet on other days the ego will chide you with, *"Really? After all these years of sitting and doing kenotic meditation, this is all you have to show for it? Pain when you sit?"*

It's gaining mind again: you'll continue to meet this on your path. *"I thought I would gain something, and I have!"* (the high), *"I'm just not gaining anything from this practice"* (the low). Perhaps the feelings won't present themselves quite like this, indeed in The Way practice it tends to be subtle variations of such feelings that mean it will take courage, discipline and devotion.

five

Practicing Kenosis
in Everyday Life

"To practice The Way is to practice Kenosis"

There are two ways you can explore "The Way" in your daily life, one as a lay follower, and the other as a more serious student of The Way. For the latter you would need to work with a teacher. While we cannot know in detail exactly what The Way comprised of for Christ's followers, we can recreate a good facsimile, one that is rooted in first century teaching and tradition but updated for our time.

Regardless of how seriously you wish to explore The Way, there are going to be common elements: reading teachings in their various forms (ancient and modern), practicing *kenosis* (self-emptying) by establishing a routine of daily contemplation, and becoming a member of a group that is also following The Way. And, again, if you wish to pursue The Way more seriously then identifying a teacher or mentor to work with will be essential.

Daily Contemplation Practice

While the Gospels do not detail the frequency with which Christ prayed, or suggested his followers pray, he was a Jew and at that time praying three times a day was standard. Whether you are looking to be a casual follower of The Way or dig far deeper into the teaching, you will want to try to establish a discipline of daily contemplation. This practice should ideally include a morning session, a midday session, and an evening session.

Many of us live very busy lives, and it may seem difficult to establish a routine that includes meditating three times a day. But if you can do so, the benefits can be disproportionately great compared to the time expended. If three sessions in a day does not fit with your schedule, then I highly recommend you at least aim for a daily routine of a morning and an evening session. That said, bear in mind that your midday session could literally be 1-5 minutes long. You may be surprised what benefits can come from even such a brief daily session and how it can immensely help cope with what the day may bring us.

However, this is not a competition to see who can meditate the longest or the most frequently. Nor does meditating several times a day, every day, make you a "better" person than those who do not. I can, though, assure you that there are significant benefits to establishing a consistent meditation practice. Thus, even if the times you set aside for contemplation are short, it is more important that you be consistent than that you find extended periods of time for your practice.

You'll see that in the above I alternated between using different words such as prayer, meditation and contemplation. This is deliberate: in The Way there needs to be recognition that each of us may have baggage associated with one or more of these terms, and thus in a sense they need to be interchangeable. You need to use the term you are most comfortable with. For some the word 'prayer' may have negative connotations of a male-centered theology, of petitionary prayer where you are asking God for things you want, so that a different term like contemplation or meditation may be more palatable.

Yet others may be triggered by terms like meditation or contemplation. We have discussed before how in the Eastern traditions refer to sessions sitting in silence as 'meditation' whereas in the West, that has often been called 'contemplation' with meditation being reserved for the act of meditating *on* something. Again, whichever terms works best for you. These are ultimately all only words; they are signifiers and essentially empty. That said, we need to be aware that certain words carry baggage or can trigger people, and I hope my using these terms interchangeably is acceptable.

As to how long to set aside for your daily practice, that will be up to you to determine what is comfortable: what works for you. As a bare minimum, your morning and evening sessions should be at least around fifteen to twenty minutes, and the midday session at least five to ten minutes. If you are able and feel called to it, then a more serious practice would involve forty-minute sessions morning and evening, and a thirty-minute session in the middle of the day.

Kenosis or Centering Prayer?

While this book focuses on kenotic meditation, I recommend you also familiarize yourself with Centering Prayer as an option, if you are not already familiar with it. Centering Prayer draws on the practice recommended in *The Cloud of Unknowing* combined with elements drawn from Buddhist meditation practices. However, we have no evidence that Christ himself had a practice that involved using such words; rather aside from the specific prayer he taught, the suggestion is that he 'prayed' in complete (internal and external) silence. This version of the practice we call *kenosis*: silent, wordless meditation/contemplation. Whether you opt for one or the other, or for a practice that mixes the two forms, is entirely up to you—the two practices are very similar.

Centering Prayer

The origin of centering prayer is associated with Fr. Thomas Keating, a Cistercian monk and former abbot of St Joseph's Abbey in Spencer, Massachusetts. In his book *Intimacy with God*, Keating acknowledges the source of the practice is in *The Cloud of Unknowing* combined with techniques he learned when sitting meditation with Zen Buddhists. He recounts how they abbey entertained a Zen master who introduced the monks to the idea of a 'sesshin'—a week-long intensive retreat. To use Fr. Keating's language, he sees Centering Prayer as choosing a word that "represents our intention to consent to God's presence and action within us." For some this language may work well, for others more non-dualistic language that affirms an aspiration to recognize (awaken to) unity might work better.

He summarizes the key elements of Centering Prayer thus:[1]

1. Choose a sacred word as a symbol of your intention to consent to God's presence and action within.
2. Sitting comfortably and with eyes closed, settle briefly and silently introduce the sacred word.
3. When you become aware of your thoughts, ever-so-gently return to the sacred word.
4. At the end of the prayer period, remain in silence with your eyes closed for a couple of minutes.

The sacred words he suggests include "God," "abba," "Jesus," and "peace." It is important, of course, that you select a word that doesn't trigger you, or cause you to start thinking. Afterall, the purpose of the chosen word is to settle the mind, not agitate it or provoke more thoughts. I am also aware that readers of this book may include non-Christians or those who may style themselves as "spiritual but not religious" (one of the fastest growing U.S. demographics) for whom the language used may be an issue.

You may thus find that words such as "now," "here," or "silence" may be better choices for you. Some have found that a variation of Psalm 46:10 works well for them—either as what they say as their sacred 'word' or what they say in preparation for sitting Centering Prayer, especially when sitting as a group:

> Be still, and know I am God
> Be still, and know I am
> Be still, and know
> Be still
> Be

Indeed, some of my students have found this works well for their midday practice: to sit quietly for a moment, then slowly say this series of words (silently or quietly out loud), and then sit for a couple minutes longer. It is quick, usually no more than five minutes in all, and yet can be a very effective dipping into the deep, refreshing well of silence within.

Practical advice on practice

Establishing a routine that you can adhere to is very important. For this reason, I do not recommend pushing yourself beyond what you are comfortable doing, since doing less on a regular basis is more important than doing more but sporadically. So, first determine how long you intend to sit for and how many times a day. And I say "intend" deliberately here, since setting intentions is a core part of The Way.

Second, establish a place you will do your practice: at home, if you can, set aside an area where you can be in quiet and not disturbed. By all means do whatever you feel comfortable doing to make this area a 'sacred space.' What that means is entirely up to you: for some it is having a comfortable chair, for others a cushion on the floor. For some it is creating a kind of altar or a table with some calming items on it such as a small flower arrangement, some item that invokes peaceful thoughts to you, perhaps a candle.

On a practical note, you will want to identify a way to time your sessions. For most of us these days this involves using the timer on our smart phone, or an app that can both time a session and have gentle sounds such as bells or bowls to mark the start and end of the period.[2] Wearing relaxing clothing can also be useful and you may wish to explore the variety of meditation and yoga clothing on sale to see if something particularly works for you.

Of course, your middle of the day session, if that is part of your daily routine, may be at work or somewhere else you have less control over where you can meditate. If possible, try to still find somewhere quiet away from others. But just go with what is possible—I have had students who are nurses or doctors and who do their midday session at their computer stations on the ward or in their breakroom. Others are able to leave their place of work and go to a nearby park, or some other place more conducive to sitting in silence. Whatever works for you.

Kenosis (Kenotic Meditation/Contemplation)

This book (and its sister volume *Christ Way*[3]) introduces an alternative to Centering Prayer, one that I believe is closer to the practice Christ himself used: I call it simply *kenosis* or Kenotic Meditation. This alternative practice is the kind I recommend for my students who wish to delve deeper into The Way. Centering Prayer can help with relaxation and, to a degree, communing with the ground of your being, but it is less likely than *kenosis* in my experience to help you realize a *metanoia* moment.[4]

Kenosis is a greater focus on self-emptying, and on being fully present to God in the moment. A single word can fill your being and completely distract you from this moment, from union with the ground of being. For this reason, we do not use words while practicing *kenosis*. The other aspect that differentiates *kenosis* from Centering Prayer is the goal of being fully awake in God in the moment, and for this reason we employ all the senses and do not close our eyes. The other reason we do not close our eyes is that this leads to a greater tendency to doze off, have a waking dream, or to just "drift."

That said, do not keep our eyes wide open either. Rather, you should have your eyes about half open, look roughly forty-five degrees down, and hold a soft gaze. This soft gaze is slightly unfocused, rather than focusing sharply on a spot on the floor or whatever is in front of you, since the idea is not to be concentrating on an object or a specific spot but rather to be fully open to all the senses.

How you sit is important, even more important for *kenosis* as you will usually be sitting for longer periods than for Centering Prayer sessions. The overriding consideration is that you sit comfortably in a way that, for you, remains comfortable for extended periods of time. You should also sit so as to promote being full awake, and for this reason you will need to sit upright, spine straight but comfortably so (don't sit such that you are straining to keep your back straight).

Your shoulders should be relaxed, and your head upright but tilted forward slightly (chin in) so that your gaze can naturally fall about forty-five degrees down. It may help to imagine a string attached to the center of the top of your head as if someone is pulling very gently on it to keep your head upright without straining to do so.

Next, we come to what you sit on, in what posture, and how you hold your hands. Because of the influence of Eastern practices, you may associate sitting for meditation as being crossed legged, on a cushion on the floor. In the East, sitting on the floor crossed

61

legged is a cultural norm in many societies. In the West this is less common since most of us are used to sitting on a chair. There is nothing inherently more "spiritual" or closer to God about sitting on a cushion on the floor, so if sitting in a chair is what works for you then that's absolutely fine. There are a number of postures that can work well:

If you are sitting crossed legged on a cushion, then there are some scientific reasons why if you're able to cross your legs fully then it can help you sit longer without back pain. You may have heard this being called "full lotus" (the first image on the left above). It does have the advantage of creating a more perfect stable triangle to help your posture during a longer period of contemplation. Second best is to cross one leg over the other (so called "half lotus"), and next best is to tuck the legs in with each other as in the upper right image (so called "Burmese" posture).

Others find kneeling to be the best for them. You can kneel on your legs but be aware this can lead to your legs "going asleep" because you're cutting off circulation to them. It is better to either sit on a small stool (see the lower left image above) or perhaps on a cushion that is stood on its side (lower middle image). Then of course is the position many in the West feel most comfortable with, sitting in a chair.

If you're sitting on a cushion, then you should sit on the edge of it so that your using a forty-five-degree angle of the cushion edge to create a more natural arch to your lower back. This also helps keep your chest open, and generally help you feel more relaxed. As I mentioned above, your shoulders should be relaxed, drawn slightly back and down. Your chin should be tucked in a little—as with other aspects of your posture, you may wish to experiment with what works best for you.

Your jaw should be free of tension so check that you are not clenching your teeth. Your tongue should be gently resting on the roof of your mouth, tip touching the back of the upper teeth. Finally, if sitting in a chair then your feet should be shoulder width apart, legs at a right angle to the floor, feet flat on the floor.

Returning to the question of your gaze for a

moment: ideally for *kenosis* you should have your eyes about half open, looking with a soft gaze about forty-five-degrees down. But if you find that, at least at first, you can relax better with your eyes closed, then do so. Ideally, in time, if you do start with your eyes closed then I would invite you to switch to opening them halfway and experiment with what difference this makes to your contemplation sessions. Again, our goal with *kenosis* is to become fully awake in God, in unity, in the moment, embodying "don't know mind."

The *Kenosis* Session

You can of course do *kenosis* on your own or in a group. Indeed, I strongly recommend finding a group to meet with on a regular basis (weekly if possible). If you are unable to find a group offering *kenosis* of Centering Prayer, then you may seek out a Zen meditation group as being the most similar. Zen meditation (also known as zazen) is also silent, and so a Zen session can be a good fit for someone practicing *kenosis*.

For your regular daily practice you have hopefully set aside an area of your house to be able to sit quietly without distraction. And as we discussed above, you have also hopefully done something to make this area a 'sacred' space in some sense of that term to you. Enter this space, or the gathering room if this is a group session, reverently as if treading on holy ground. Since, in a real sense, that is what you are doing.

Facing your chair of cushion, put your hands together as if in prayer, chest level, and make a slight bow of reverence to your chair or cushion.

Then turn round with your back to the chair or cushion, retaining your praying hand position, and make a slight bow again. On your own this is to the room (or to the universe); in a group this is to the other sitting in contemplation with you. Now, gently sit and get yourself comfortable. At this point when sitting on your own you will be setting the timer for your session; in a group someone will have been assigned this task.

Having settled into a comfortable position, take a moment to run a mental check of all the points above regarding your posture, how you are sitting, relax your shoulders, make sure your tongue is gently in the roof of your mouth, tip resting lightly on the back of your top front teeth. Now take a few deep breaths: breath slowly and deeply from your belly area, not shallow breaths from your chest. It may help to count slowly to five as you breath in, then hold your breath for five, and breath out for five ("one one-thousand, two one-thousand ... etc. to ... five one thousand"). During the session, though, you should be to breath naturally—this is not a "yoga style" practice that involves deep breathing or controlled breathing techniques.

As you sit the goal can be summed up by "Let go and let God." In a real sense, you are aiming to get yourself (the "self" with a small "s") out of the way and become a non-judgmental presence, becoming fully awake to the moment just as it is. As the joke goes, *"God, I prayed to you every day, all day long, and you never answered me!"* to which God responds, *"That's because I couldn't get a word in edge-wise!"*

As Meister Eckhart put it, *"There is a huge silence inside each of us that beckons us into itself, and the recovery of our own silence can begin to teach us the language of heaven."*

Our goal with *kenosis* isn't to stop our thoughts, but as thoughts come up just observe them like clouds and let them float by. As Shunryu Suzuki wisely said: *"[When meditating] leave your front door and your back door open. Let thoughts come and go. Just don't serve them tea."* The same goes for feelings and emotions: if they arise, just watch them and try not to be triggered by them or let them start your thinking processes.

Now, if you are like most people, letting your thoughts just float by is far easier said than done. For many, thoughts rampage through us constantly, moving from one thought to another at a quick pace. Or we have a pattern of thoughts that we keep going round and round on, in a vicious circle that seems hard to break. *"Did I remember to turn the stove off?" "I wonder if I have time to go to the gas station on the way to my next meeting?" "What if I hadn't said that thing to him, maybe he would still be speaking to me..."* And so on. We call this *monkey mind.*

Whereas in Centering Prayer we seek to calm our thoughts by repeating a word to ourselves, in *kenosis* we focus on non-verbal means that do not use words that could trigger further thoughts. For instance, a standard method to rein in monkey mind is to count breaths. What I recommend is to start counting your breaths with a count of one for a complete cycle of in-breath and out-breath, then continue to count to ten. When you get to ten, I recommend starting at one again rather than counting on up to higher numbers. Then, when your thoughts have quietened down a little, try returning to not counting and just breathing naturally.[5]

Just like learning a new physical exercise routine, *kenosis* can take time to accustomed to, but you will improve significantly with experience. With persistence and by establishing a regular daily routine you will be able to get to a point where counting breaths is no longer necessary.

Indeed, one of the major benefits to *kenosis* over Centering Prayer is that by focusing on open-eyed, wordless silent contemplation we can more easily transfer this practice into our every-day life.

Ultimately, it becomes possible to practice *kenosis* not just for limited periods in a special space but be in mindful unity with God in all that you do throughout each day. A practice not dissimilar to that advocated by the seventeenth century French monk, Brother Lawrence, in his work *The Practice of the Presence of God*.[6]

You might wish to start your meditation session with something that you say—either out loud (particularly if you are in a group) or silently to yourself. This may be a prayer or words that you find helpful to center you ready for a contemplative session. For instance, you may wish to use the variation based on Psalm 26 above. Or, as Christ instructed, you may wish to say what has become known as "The Lord's Prayer." I am aware, though, that this prayer runs the gamut for people from being a central part of their faith to something that people have issues with due to the male-centered wording.

The prayer is not in the Gospel of Mark, but two versions of it appear in both Matthew and Luke. This has led scholars to speculate that its origins are in the speculated missing source text "Q" which is thought to mainly be a collection of Christ's sayings. It does not, however, appear in any other text such as the Gospel of Thomas which is otherwise thought to resemble "Q." Thomas does consistently refer to God, or the supreme being, as "father."

For some, referring to God as he, or indeed as Father, is problematic for various reasons. God is beyond labels, beyond male and female, and thus not a "he." In more recent times others have pointed out that for some who have a negative view of a father—perhaps they were abused by their father, or their father left them—it may be difficult to have the ground of being or higher power referred to as father, or even as male.

Despite Paul having not met Jesus, and thus not getting his teachings accurate, there are some "gems" within his letters. For instance, in Galatians Paul says that God does not use a mediator because "God is one," (3:20) and that in Christ[7] "there is neither Jew nor Gentile...nor is there male and female" (3:28). And of course, we have Christ himself teaching that everyone is everyone else's brother and sister so long as their will is aligned with God's will (by which they enter the Kingdom of Heaven and become a Son of God/Daughter of God).

While it is understandable that there has been a growing pushback against the use of male terms for God, on the other hand there is poetry in Christ's metaphor of the need to be born again of Water/God (the spiritual Father) and Spirit (the feminine aspect of God, God as Mother, Sophia/Wisdom). One approach—used by many progressive churches—is to convert all male references to God to neutral language, but while it has merit this can lose a key part of Christ's message.

For this reason, in order to retain the metaphor so central to Christ's teachings, I would recommend using both Father and Mother rather than going gender neutral in our language. That said, it is equally important to bear in mind that God is beyond sex, beyond gender and thus in instances where it does not make sense to add both Father and Mother (Abba and Amma in Aramaic) it will be more appropriate to use neutral language stripped of any suggestion God is male. In short, use the wording that works best for you, but bear in mind that words can be powerful—both in their impact on you and on others—so use them mindfully with an eye on the consequence of their use.

That all being said, I'd draw your attention back to a key teaching of The Way: to fully awaken, and that includes fully awaking to both the absolute and the relative. Absolute views of God include God is infinite, God is everywhere, God is everything, God is nothing ("no-thing"), everyone/everything is God, and so on. Relative language includes God as Father, God as Mother, God as anything (that is, any language that implies a dualistic view of God as separate from you, separate from any*thing* or any*one*), and so on. In following this path of The Way, you will be fully exploring all of this. The intellect is a useful tool, but it can also be a seductive, deceitful enemy on the path to Truth.

A few more comments here on the language of

God: first century Middle Eastern culture was male dominated. Thus, it would have been natural to talk of God as being Love (not as being lov*ing*) and that this Love—*agápe* not *éros*—is like the exceptionally unselfish love a father has for his only begotten son. In more recent times, especially in the West, it might have become more usual to liken this absolute unselfish "Love" as being like that of a mother for her only child.

But even this can be seen as a feature of a male-dominated society that limits the role of to being in the role of child-bearer, mother, housewife and so on. In our more enlightened time we can now understand this extreme unselfish love is like that of any parent for their only child, be those parents male and female, both male, both female, or whatever other gender or sexual identification or orientation the parent(s) may identify with (be there two parents or one parent).

When all else is stripped away—our ego-based view of the world, the world of dualism, and we fully integrate the absolute and the relative—what remains is Love. In Buddhist terms what is left is compassion since most Buddhists prefer the term compassion to a concept of unselfish love. This Love—this pure compassion—is who you truly are. It is your True Self, your Christ-nature.

Following the path of The Way

While silent time in your secluded place is central

to your practice in this Way, the full teaching has several stages on your journey to Unity. Studying the core teachings, stripped of the post-Easter Jesus language that was added at a later date, should also be central to your path. And as I have mentioned before, this part of your path is best pursued with a teacher or mentor.[8]

The Seven Stations of The Way (or the Seven 'Demons')

If you have spent any length of time studying first century Wisdom Tradition texts and Jewish teachings of that era, you will have noticed how important certain numbers are. In particular the numbers three and seven. Thus, when we read that Mary Magdalene was someone Christ had helped overcome seven demons, we know there is something symbolic in this statement by the use of the number seven.

In Jewish culture of the first century, three was the number of holiness and love. Hence, twelve was seen as the number for union of the people with God being the product of three and four (it was not coincidental that Christ was said to have twelve disciples). And seven, being the sum of three and four, was the symbol most associated with all aspects of God: acts of atonement and purification always involved seven sprinklings of water. Most pertinent here, seven was the divine number of completion. Hence to rid someone of seven demons meant to complete something divine with that person, here almost certainly completing a course of teachings, achieving unity.

In various texts we have repeated mention that Mary Magdalene was Christ's most favored disciple, and that she "got" his teachings in a way the other disciples did not. In ancient teachings that substantially pre-date the time of Jesus, a spiritual journey was said to have seven stages (also known as "stations"): Intention, self-examination, atonement, initial awakening (*metanoia*), oneness (the heart of the secret), the station of freedom (attachment to freedom), and finally The Truth (the Absolute, nonattachment thinking, "this just as it is").

In the context of first century Palestine culture it is entirely possible that this is what was referred to as the demons that Mary Magdalene was relieved of. Each station is like demon, in that archaic sense of the term: something you need to expunge. But in reality, nothing is gained, nothing is expunged. Eyes are made one, and opened wide, veils are lifted (there never were veils).

Station 1: Intention

This initial stage is just as simple as it sounds, it is just a matter of setting the intention to fully and completely follow the path of The Way. There is a strong element of discernment in this first phase: is this the right path for you? Is it a good fit for you? During this first phase you will be identifying a teacher or mentor to work with. I cannot emphasize enough how important finding a good teacher can be. Visit the website for this book (www.kenosisbook.com) for help in this.

Circle of The Way

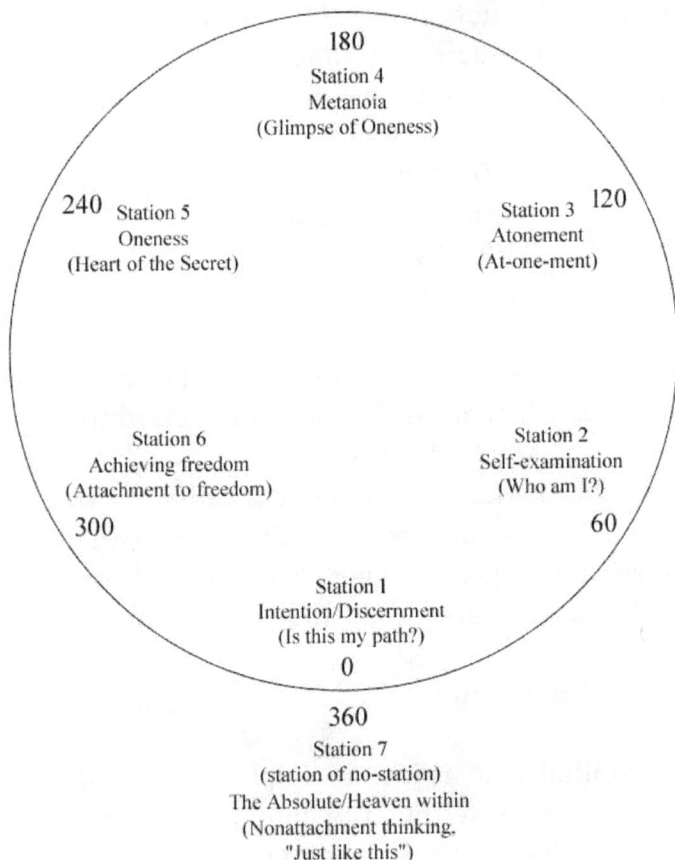

180
Station 4
Metanoia
(Glimpse of Oneness)

240 Station 5
Oneness
(Heart of the Secret)

Station 3 120
Atonement
(At-one-ment)

Station 6
Achieving freedom
(Attachment to freedom)
300

Station 2
Self-examination
(Who am I?)
60

Station 1
Intention/Discernment
(Is this my path?)
0

360
Station 7
(station of no-station)
The Absolute/Heaven within
(Nonattachment thinking.
"Just like this")

An essential part of this first phase is also setting the clear intention to have helping others be central to your life. If you do not already have some way in which you are helping others as part of your everyday life, then seek a way to start doing so—either by volunteering your time or by a change of profession. Core to who you truly are is "How may I help you?" and from this first phase onwards you will be seeking ways to uncover this truth in your life.

Station 2: Self-Examination

This phase is a deep dive into the question "Who am I?" in all its meanings and consequences. It is also a reflection on what the word "God" means to you, or what a different term (such as higher power, ground of being, palpable presence, etc.) means to you. These questions are related, of course, since the question "Who am I?" includes who do you perceive your 'self' to be (with a small s) and your 'Self' (with a large S), your true self? What do these terms mean to you? Again, having a teacher or mentor can be invaluable.

To truly know yourself is to know God: how this counter-intuitive phrase make senses is part of what The Way is all about. Thus, discerning perfectly who you are in this phase is not the goal, rather it is to take this deep dive and see how far you get. Like many things on a spiritual path, this exploration of "Who am I?" will remain a core part of your practice on an ongoing basis, as will cultivating a state of *metanoia*.

The more fully you explore your self in this phase the more you will benefit from the practice going forward. Be aware, though, that our intellect and our ego are remarkably good at placing blinders on our eyes. We see what we want to see, and what we imagine others see when they look at us. So, start with absolute basics: How tall are you? How old are you? What is your gender? How would you describe yourself and how do you believe others would describe you? What would you say are your main qualities and strengths? What are your least attractive qualities and your weaknesses?

If you haven't done so, consider finding out what your enneagram type is, and if you can take a personality test such as the Myers-Briggs. Do you agree with the results? If not, why not? Would you describe yourself as a caring person? If not, why do you think that might be? What would you consider your major sins to be, both past and present? And here I use the term sin in its broadest sense—go beyond what you believe you have been taught the word 'sin' to mean, and consider it to be anything that is other that your will being aligned with God's will.

This can be murky water, down in the mud and weeds, for most of us. So be gentle with yourself. The idea of this phase isn't to itemize all that is bad about yourself and then beat yourself up for it. Focus equally on your good qualities as much as you are tempted to focus on your 'bad' ones. And above all, focus on what you really find to be true, right here right now, in this moment. Not on what you have been told is true, or the image or your 'self' that has been constructed by others or by society. That said, ask those closest to you to give a candid summary of how they see you, your strengths and weaknesses. Consider this a fact-finding tour: you are not trying to give yourself a home brewed psychotherapy session: this is about dispassionately, objectively itemizing everything you can respond to the question "Who am I?"

Station 3: Atonement (at-one-ment)

To the casual observer looking at Christianity from outside, it may appear to be a generally pleasant religion that promotes a range of good conduct coupled with an overarching call to love one another. Nothing too deep or terribly spiritual, just a guide for how to live a good life. What makes this exterior simplified view of Christianity so widely believed is the post-Easter Jesus fabrication of the sin-based theology that Christ himself did not teach.

Stated most simply, this invented theology says that if you don't repent your sins then you won't go to a place called "heaven" after you die. But if you do repent your sins then your entry to this afterlife is assured. And in many cases the concept of "original sin" gets added, ensuring that you get off to a bad start in life by being born a sinner because of what Adam and Eve did. Saint Augustine has a lot to answer for in this aspect of the post-Easter Jesus invention.

I've discussed elsewhere that this sin-based theology is derived partly from an appalling error in translating the Greek word *metanoia* as "repent" and a failure to grasp what Christ was teaching when he spoke of "heaven within." This is not to say that Christ didn't teach that to sin was wrong or that you shouldn't repent your sins. However, what constitutes "sin" in Christ's teachings? At one extreme, the answer is anything you do that is your will rather than God's will. This is an accurate statement, but hardly helpful for most people since aligning your will with God's will is, as Christ taught, the narrow door through which few pass.

On a more granular level, it is not obeying the ten commandments, or not obeying the new commandment to love God and to "Love your neighbor as yourself" (Matt 12:31). This second part of Christ's new commandment is actually the same as his teaching to align your will with God's will. There is a tendency to add in words that are not there in Christ's teaching: to read it as if it says "Love your neighbor as you would love yourself" or "Love your neighbor as you would have them love you"—which is not what it says.

Rather, it is a commandment that is really a deep teaching of interdependence. A teaching of non-duality that says the other is you, and you are the other. It is a call to love others being aware that they *are* your self. Your true self is not separate from lots of other selves, but rather is a unity. And this is the "Love" that he teaches that God "is"—hence to love another recognizing that they are your self is to align your will with God's will and become a Son/Daughter of God.

But this takes us full circle, since to say that sin is

failure to align your will with God's will is no more useful than to say that sin is a failure to appreciate the non-duality inherent in loving all others with the recognition that they are you. When asked most people would say that their concept of "sin" goes beyond failing to adhere to the ten commandments or failing to adhere to the commandment to love their neighbor.

Yet, Christ's teachings do not give much further granularity as to what constitutes right action, right conduct, right speech, right thought, and so on. Instead, the Church has tended to guide people toward priests to tell them what is or is not a sin, thus keeping mainstream church and the priesthood in control of the definition of "sin." This is not helpful to followers of The Way since by our nature we are not drawn to formalized religion with strict hierarchies where clerics tell us what to do and what not to do, where male-based language dominates, or where the purpose of the hierarchy is, or appears to be, to control church members or to be driven by financial gain.

The following vows or commitments assist in our clarifying the ethical guidelines we adhere to as followers of The Way. Some bear a resemblance to the Ten Commandments, but with added nuance and subtlety[9]:

I vow to not kill, but rather to encourage and cultivate life.
I vow not to take what is not freely given to me, but

rather to cultivate and encourage generosity.

I vow not to misuse sexuality and instead to remain faithful in relationships.

I vow not to lie or speak dishonestly, but rather to promote truthful communication.

I vow not to become intoxicated but rather to polish clarity and dispel delusions.

I vow not to slander others, but rather to encourage respectful speech.

I vow not to praise myself above others, rather to promote modesty and lift others up where appropriate.

I vow not to be greedy, either with wealth and material things, but also with understanding and teachings.

I vow not to harbor ill-will or anger, but rather promote equanimity, harmony and selfless kindness.

I vow to be conscious of what I consume, the way in which it was produced, and what harm might result from my consuming it. I vow to bring awareness.

This of course isn't an attempt at an exhaustive list of vows you might consider adhering to. But it is a good core to carry with you as a key part of your walking on The Way. In this phase we do a deep dive into our ethical behavior and an honest introspection of our less than perfect behavior. This process does not work, though, unless you are entirely honest with yourself.

Having identified areas of your life that could use some improvement (remember Suzuki "*You are perfect as you are, but you could use some improvements*"), the next step is atonement. This word, often equated with "repentance," literally translates to "at-one-ment" which is important to us on The Way, since this is precisely our goal. It has at least two meanings: to be at one with this whole big mess we call our lives, and to be at one with God in the sense of constantly vowing to bring our will into line with God's will. Helping us on this journey is a short verse of atonement that we shall be using:

> *All evil thoughts and actions by me since of old,*
> *because of my beginningless greed, anger, and*
> *ignorance,*
> *born of my body, mouth and thought,*
> *now I atone for it all.*

Now you will note some unusual language here. The use of "since of old" and "beginningless ..." this is because as we follow this path of The Way we come to realize that we are all connected. We "inter-are" as Thich Nhat Hanh says.[10] A crucial part of this station is the appreciation that you are not an island, you are not a separate "thing" in a world of separate "things." In assessing your own issues, you come to find that they are both yours and not yours. That what others do is what you do since there is no "you" and "them"—that is dualistic thinking conning you into a false belief that you are separate and distinct from the universe, from God.

Thus, we bring forward into this phase what we developed in the first phase: the "by me" in the first

81

line above should constantly have you harking back to "Who am I?" or in this case "What does me mean here?" And this greed, anger, ignorance, is it "mine" or is it shared with all sentient beings? All 'children of God' (to borrow Christ's phrase)? If my brother or sister (and here we recall who Christ says your brother and sister are) act badly or speak badly, there is no "they" who are wrong and no "I" who is right. Certainly, there are actions, words, thoughts that I am in direct control of, but we are not separate from others. What any one of us does, thinks, says, is what we all do, think, say.

Station 4: *Metanoia*

In this phase you will double-down on cultivating a "beginner's mind" or "don't know mind:" a state of perceiving, acting and being arising from before thought. This is God's mind, complete beginner's mind, not the "I know it all" mind of the typical human being. This is also known as *shoshin* in the Japanese Zen tradition, and refers to having an attitude of eagerness, openness, and a lack of preconceptions. As simple as this might sound, it can be remarkably difficult to cultivate this beginner's mind, this "don't know mind."

In this phase you will be focused on meditation (Centering Prayer or *Kenosis*, or what other practice works for you). You will also be focused on reading deeply but selectively, and at all times asking yourself "What is this?" and then immediately answering to yourself "Don't know." You will also continue to ask yourself "Who am I?" since this reflection will never be exhausted while you follow this path of The Way.

This phase concludes when you have experienced at least one instance of *metanoia* (the "ah ha!" moment or glimpse of awakening), or when your teacher or mentor believes you are ready.

Station 5: Oneness

You've had a moment of awakening to oneness, and whether by direct ongoing experience or by intellect, you now "get" that you are one with everything, one with God. Your true self, the Self with a capital S, is infinite and not subject to live and death. The true you, having glimpsed heaven within, knows you have been around since beginningless time. Everyone who has ever existed, everyone who will ever exist, are all present in this moment.

It is a deep, profound realization, but one that can be seductive and deceptive. It is not unusual for those who experience this astounding awareness of oneness to believe "That's it! I've done it! I've overcome the ego and become one with God!" Or more simply, "I've experienced oneness, so that's the end of this spiritual path. I'm home." Of course, nothing could be further from the truth.

Rather, this is the station where you real work begins. This station is also known as the *Heart of the Secret* because in a sense it is the heart of what we seek in discovering heaven within and entering what Christ called "The Kingdom." So, here you are, born again of Water and the Spirit (God the Father and God the Mother, your spiritual parents). Now is the time to learn what it is to live this new life, reincarnated as you are, in your spiritual rebirth, in the body of a human being.

If you think you overcame the ego, destroyed the ego, fully entered non-dual perception and overcame all dualistic perception, then you have indeed deluded yourself. What then do you find as you explore this new 'you' (which is absolutely no different from the old you), this spiritually reborn 'you?' The danger here is becoming addicted to this oneness, addicted to the idea of 'being pure spirit.'

One thing you may discover in this phase is what we call Freedom. But this isn't freedom as you usually think of it, it is a more dangerous, very seductive freedom. A freedom that feels God-like: "There's nothing I can't do now that I am spiritually reborn, awake in God."

Station 6: The Seduction of Freedom

This is the phase that Christ experienced in the desert for 40 days following his awakening at his baptism by John the Baptist. The description of what Christ allegedly experienced in that time in the desert is an almost perfect example of what Zen Master Seung Sahn called "270" on his compass, and what we call

"300" on our Circle of The Way.

Here you have broken through your addiction to oneness, to the idea of no form (just being spirit) and realize the deep sense of freedom that will come from this breakthrough. The ego already jumped in during station 5: "You're so great! Very few people have a true *metanoia* experience! You've achieved spiritual greatness!" Now, the ego enters even more assiduously, one last gasp attempt to regain control of your mind, your being.

In the Gospels, the so-called temptation of Christ is the narrative in all three synoptic Gospels detailing his experience in the desert of 40-days after his baptism by John. The language used is that of Satan (remember, that is *natas*, life, backwards) tempting him while Christ was fasting and meditating on the experience of awakening he had. His major *metanoia* moment as he rose from the water.

In these temptations Christ is encouraged to use his new powers to turn stones into bread. Then he is encouraged to jump from the highest point of the temple and show that he will land below unhurt. Next, he is taken to the highest nearby mountain and told that all this that you can see will be yours if you would just worship "me" and not God.

These are a near perfect description of the kind of experiences someone will experience in this station 6. Replace the word "Satan" with "ego" and it becomes somewhat clearer what is happening here. Although we talk of this station as being associated with freedom, another word for it is power. And power is seductive: absolute power corrupts absolutely, as the saying goes. And there is no power greater than that of the divine ground of your being.

In this phase people have reported experiencing what they can only describe as 'powers' such as the ability to foresee the future, the ability to heal others, and other inexplicable abilities. Still others have reported a sense of having such power, but not of experiencing any actual evidence of it. The sensation of it is sometimes all it takes for the ego to convince you that you are some kind of God. As your realization of your True Self, your Christ nature, is coming close the ego tries all it can in one last desperate attempt to prevent that.

This can be particularly true if you appear to others as what they describe as "charismatic," the kind of personality that having experienced *metanoia* then finds people are very drawn to them. And that people having been drawn to them tend to do whatever the 'master' (teacher, guru, etc.) suggests they do. That can be a very seductive sensation to have that degree of power over others.

Station 7: the station of no station, The Absolute, Unity

This is home, and it is exactly where you started:

appropriately depicted as 360 on the circle, exactly where zero is and the point of your departure on this path of The Way. Here is the mature and full integration of the infinite (the absolute) and the finite (the relative). The final answer to the question "Who am I?" in all its nuances and levels of truth.

This is where you rest in the mind of God, living the reality of "thy will not my will be done." This is the station of "just like this" nothing is other than just as it is. Here is the awareness of being fully human and fully divine, of what it means to be both a Son of Man (the term the Jews used for a human being) and a Son of God (of Daughter of Man/Daughter of God). This is the realm of nonattachment thinking, this is the realm of non-dualism with full and deep awareness of dualism, too.

It is also the phase of which even this is already too much said since it is the realm best conveyed in silence. But it is not a station you have arrived at. It is not a final phase you have "achieved." You are exactly where you have always been, one with God. Fully human and fully divine. Home.

Some final thoughts on putting it all into practice in everyday life:

Find a Teacher or Mentor

Find a teacher or mentor to walk this journey with you, one that fully understands this path of The Way described in this book. Also seek out a local group if you possibly can where you can regularly practice either Centering Prayer or *Kenosis* and become part of a like-minded community of seekers on The Way. You may be able find assistance with this by visiting the website for this book (www.kenosisbook.com) or the main website for StillCenter (www.stillcenter.org).

Seek Liminal Space(s)

The term *liminal space* has been used in various ways, but here I am talking about the hard to describe sense that there are places or circumstances where the veils between us and unity with God are thinner. For some this can be when they walk in the woods, spend time in nature, or perhaps when they climb a mountain. I don't think it is a coincidence that there is repeated reference to Christ retreating to his solitary place, or ascending a nearby mountain to pray.

I invite you to find your liminal space: that place where you feel the spiritual air is rarified, the veils are thinner or fewer, a place where there is a greater sense of a palpable presence.

---

[1] Keating, Thomas (1994) *Intimacy with God*. Crossroad Publishing: NY. p 64
[2] There are many such apps, but one I have found good is *Insight Timer*.
[3] Tim Langdell, *Christ Way, Buddha Way: Jesus as Wisdom Teacher and a Zen Perspective on His Teachings*, StillCenter Publications, 2020
[4] But a note of caution here: what will bring about a *metanoia* experience for someone is unpredictable. Some may follow a strict practice for many years and then it is an off-hand comment by a co-worker, or an inane tagline for a product advertisement, something random, that triggers the "ah ha!" that is *metanoia*. Teachers, including

Christ, can only suggest a series of practices, The Way, that have been shown to be more likely than not to help someone experience *metanoia*.
[5] Counting breaths uses words. Don't get hung up on this, since to count breaths is the training wheels of this practice. After a while you will not need to do this.
[6] Brother Lawrence (1692) *The Practice of the Presence of God: with Christian Meditation Practice Guide by Tim Langdell*. StillCenter Publications: Pasadena (2020, updated, modern language version).
[7] Paul uses this term "in Christ" 170 times in his letters, although he never clarifies what he means by it. Just as he uses the term "Christ Jesus" whereas the Gospel writers tend to use "Jesus Christ."
[8] If you wish to learn more about these post-Easter Jesus additions and amendments to the gospels, then I recommend the sister volume *Christ Way, Buddha Way*.
[9] These vows draw on various religious groups and Zen centers, all of which are hereby acknowledged, with gratitude.
[10] Thich Nhat Hanh (2020) *Interbeing, 4th Edition: The 14 Mindfulness Trainings of Engaged Buddhism* (reprint edition) Parallax Press.

six

Meditation: A Deeper Dive

Those who have practiced meditation for a number of years often forget how difficult it was for them when they first started. I recall how when I was attending seminary one of our professors started her class by asking everyone to close their eyes and sit meditatively for just five minutes.

When the five minutes were up, she struck a small "singing bowl" and gently asked the class. "How did you find that experience?

My fellow students mostly responded that they found it very calming and peaceful. To my surprise, around half the class commented that they had they had never done that, or anything like it, before. I was shocked, since in the world I move in it is common to meditate. I made a mental note to bear in mind that many people do not meditate nor do they even take a few minutes to sit in silence with their eyes closed—let alone to meditate *kenosis* style with their eyes partly open.

The professor also asked the class how long they thought the silence had lasted for. The responses were all over the map: "It was about forty-five seconds," said one student, "Must have been at least ten minutes," said another. Well over half the class were surprised to learn it was five minutes. This suspension of our usual skills at judging the passage of time are common in meditation practice. I've lost count of the number of times someone has said to me after a forty-minute session, "I was sure the timekeeper had fallen asleep and forgotten to ring the bell!"

What the professor said next has stayed with me: she recounted how she had done the same process around a year earlier she had once again asked her class to close their eyes and had them sit for give minutes. When she hit the singing bell to end the brief session, one student said, "Teacher! Don't you ever do that to me again!" The student went on to complain that sitting in silence for five minutes with her eyes closed was, hands-down, the worst experience of her entire life.

If you experience challenges when you try to meditate, please be reassured this is entirely normal. The practice of meditation should never be seen as a competition: just because another person can sit fully cross-legged (in "full lotus") for hours on end, and seem completely calm and still, does not make that person a "better meditator" than you if you cannot do that. That said, I have known many people who have mastered sitting in a good, formal posture, perfectly still, who when asked will report that despite appearing calm and serene their mind is in fact constantly raging with out of control thoughts (what we call "monkey mind).

Like any practice—whether it's running a marathon, lifting weights or developing any other skill—it is entirely normal to start slowly and build your skills. Meditation practice takes persistence, perseverance, and determination. This is another reason that I highly recommend that you establish a regular routine of meditation practice, even if it is only for a short period a couple of times day. Like skill, you will become more and more accomplished in time.

If you sit with others you may find the challenges greater than when you sit alone at home. It is not at all unusual for beginning practitioners to be self-conscious at first when they sit in a group setting. Suddenly, it feels as if your breath is loud, and even your heartbeat is deafening. It may almost seem embarrassing that just sitting in total silence causes you to somehow forget how to breath properly. This is the centipede's dilemma:

> *A centipede was happy – quite!*
> *Until a toad in fun*
> *Said, "Pray, which leg comes after which?"*
> *Which threw her mind in such a pitch,*
> *She laid bewildered in the ditch*
> *Considering how to run.*

If you experience this, don't worry, it's not at all unusual at first to become self-conscious about basic processes like breathing. For others it is swallowing, they find saliva building up in their mouth as they sit because they are "forgetting" to swallow. Zazen can be an excellent litmus test for one's current state of mind: if you can sit and *just sit*, breathing normally, you have taken an important first step toward effortless sitting. A lucky few have no such problems from the beginning, others start with no problems and then as their sitting deepens the issues arise: *"That tickle in my throat! But they said not to cough in group..."*; *"Oh no, now my face is itching, should I scratch it? Will someone be annoyed if I move my hand?"*

Some effort is necessary to get past any such initial issues, but above all be gentle on yourself. You will get to a point where *kenosis* is effortless, but it will take time and patience. Remember, the best way to make cloudy water clear is to just leave it alone.

"Flail in the water and you will drown,
relax and you will float"

Kenosis—self-emptying—is not about learning something, it is about unlearning. You will be surprised just how many habits, beliefs, constructs and assumptions you have acquired in the few years you have been alive. Whether you are eighteen or ninety-eight, you have accumulated a huge number of deep-rooted ideas about who you are and what the universe is all about. Take your basic everyday view of the world: looking around the room you are in, it is full of color, right? Now look straight ahead without moving your head and notice the room to your left and to your right. Far left, far right. You don't feel you are in a room that is a mix of color and monochrome, right?

But the fact is you see color with the center of your eyes, whereas your peripheral vision is attuned to perceiving movement. It makes sense in evolutionary terms since being able to see detail and colors is more important in the center of your visual field that you are focused on. Whereas it is more important that you be aware of someone or something creeping up on you, so movement sensors are more important at the edges of your sight.

Yet you don't perceive the world as being color immediately ahead of you and grey everywhere else, rather you live in a colorful world. This is because your brain is filling in the color and creating your perception of a world that has continuity and coherence. Where coherence doesn't exist (in the sense of actual perceptual data being received by the brain), the brain fills in the gaps.

It is well known that so-called "eyewitnesses" are notoriously unreliable. Five people seeing the same person commit the same act have been known to give five quite different accounts. Person one expected to see someone of a specific demographic and so that is what they see. Person two expected to see a different kind of person, and so that is what they see. There is a video on the Internet of some people playing with a ball. Over and again, when asked to watch the video and count the number of times the ball bounces people have the same reaction. They are totally stunned to later learn that while they watched the ball, a man in a gorilla suit had walked across the screen, totally unnoticed by them. On replaying the video, they find it hard to believe they missed such an obvious thing the first viewing.

More often than we realize, we see what we expect to see rather than some raw unprocessed perception of the world just as it really is. Perhaps you've had an experience in twilight hours when you see a dog in the leaves beneath the tree, only to then realize what you are looking at is just the wind churning up the leaves.

Again, this makes sense that our brain makes stuff up: every millisecond thousands of new pieces of sense data enter our senses. We can't handle processing absolutely every piece of sense data, and it isn't necessary for us to function in the world that we do so. Indeed, as the autistic person can attest, if you do try to process all your sense data you can freeze up with processing overload.

There's a very good reason why Christ taught that to enter the Kingdom of Heaven (within) you need to become like a little child. A child who is still filled with wonder and hasn't been conditioned by society to see this but not that, to think this but not that, to react this way but not that way, etc. But to become functioning adults we must become conditioned, we have to develop both conceptions and preconceptions because they help us to stay safe, to survive. If having touched a hot stove burner and felt the pain we do not develop a concept of "glowing stove burners are hot" then we keep touching the burner, keep getting burnt.

That may sound trivial, but it isn't. Such concepts and preconceptions can be practical, but they can also be perfidious and insidious. We need to learn that objects that get larger and larger are coming toward us. If we fail to integrate this into our basic perception of the world then we get run over by the Mack truck. But these concepts and preconceptions are at their most subtle and tricky when it comes to the ego.

Now, you may have been told that non-dual contemplative practices are all about "destroying your ego," but this is nonsense. It depends what you mean by the word "ego" of course, but regardless, nothing about this practice involves destruction of ego. If you mean your sense of self as a separate being, separate from all other beings, then your path includes recognizing that this is a delusion. But if you mean the "me" who says while standing in the middle of the road, *"That shape coming toward me is getting larger every moment,"* then you had certainly better not destroy it. Remember the Mack truck.

In this moment you are absolutely finite and small, but you are also infinite and limitless. This is the relative and the absolute we discussed before. But the relative is the absolute—it is all you, the finite and the infinite. You are x-feet, y-inches tall (the *relative*); and you are no size at all, you are infinitely large (the *absolute*). Realizing this calls for cultivating a pure mind. This pure mind is the "beginner's mind" (what Christ meant by the mind of a child—not child*ish* but child*like*) it is to be constantly saying to yourself *"What is this? Don't know."* It is holding a don't know mind, it is dwelling in non-dualism when the entirety of our life seems to scream for us to dwell in dualism.

If you seek the secret of heaven on the top of a mountain, then the only secret of heaven you'll find there is the one you brought with you. Similarly, you will be disappointed if you attend a meditation group and assume that act alone will give you oneness with God. Much of the problem is the basic teaching of *kenosis* is that you need to wake up and realize your true self, but you don't understand that concept: *"Surely I'm already awake? I woke up this morning, and have been awake all day ever since, haven't I?"* As hard as it may be to envisage going to sleep and never waking up, how much harder is it to imagine waking up when you never fell asleep?

There is a good reason why when someone experiences an awakening experience (often called a "mystical experience") it can be accompanied by a feeling of elation, light-headedness, even ecstasy. Now, here lies the danger: having experienced that moment, having felt ecstatic, you can then be tempted to spend years trying to "get back" to *that* experience. The seduction, the error, is to believe that the "high" you experience in an awakening moment is the goal. The mistake is thinking that this is the feeling a fully awakened person experiences all the time. This way lies the danger of being attracted to mind altering substances since they may be a way of recreating such "highs," but they are an illusion and take one further and further away from realizing your true self.

To discourage being too tempted by such "highs", some teachers will say "The Kingdom of Heaven is as grey as grey." Of course, saying the ultimate goal is an utterly grey world view is hardly a great selling point! Indeed, it isn't true: when awake, when you develop no-dual perception and realize your true self, grey is just grey, startling red is just startling red, pain is pain—but it isn't suffering. Ecstasy is ecstasy—but it isn't seductive.

For many, having a mystical experience of oneness with God, or even just a momentary glimpse of non-dual consciousness, is as much a curse as a gift. If it leads to a belief that the initial buzz you got is the state you need to return to, then indeed it can be a curse since that is not what awakening is all about. It can also be dispiriting: I have lost count of the people who have said to me, "*I had what I thought was a mystical experience many years ago, but I've never been able to get it again.*"

For many, one may struggle to see some of Christ's parables as anything other than nonsense until one experiences at least a glimpse of non-dual consciousness: then it all starts to make sense. An *"Ah ha!"* moment happens for most and this is the point it can be so very important that a student of *kenosis* and *metanoia* has a teacher or mentor to guide them through processing the experience. Without such guidance, it can be easy to fall into the trap that the emotions felt are seen as the main goal of *kenosis* that must be experienced again.

"When all else falls away,
> *what remains is compassion"*

I do not recommend playing the game of "spot the enlightened being," but should you be tempted to look for someone who is on the path, then do not look for the person always happy, always laughing (even when sad events occur), but rather look for that person with a gentle smile, one who laughs heartily when appropriate, and cries freely when appropriate, has an unassuming air, an unselfish nature, and a presence of equanimity—nothing seems to unsettle them.

Your true nature is compassion: may you realize it.

ABOUT THE AUTHOR

Born in Oxford, England, Tim Langdell is both ordained as a Christian Priest in the Independent Catholic Church (in communion with the Episcopal Church) and a Master Zen Teacher. He is also a member of a Thomasine Order (an order of monks and priests centered on the Gospel of Thomas). He became passionate about both Zen and Mystical Christianity at age 19, when he had what he would now describe as a mystical experience, of oneness with God. He became a life-professed member of the Anglican *Third Order of St. Francis* around that time, too.

Tim has lived in Pasadena, California since around 1990, while spending time in his beloved Oxford whenever he can. Tim gained his MDiv at Claremont School of Theology where he also studied at Bloy House Episcopal Seminary. He also holds a PhD in clinical psychology from University College, London, an MA in Educational and Clinical Child Psychology from Nottingham University, and a BS (known in the UK as a BSc) in Physics and Psychology from Leicester University.

He is the rector of Church of the Beloved Disciple as well as Abbot and Guiding Teacher at the Pasadena Zen Center (known as StillCenter), too. Tim is a Board-Certified Chaplain, having gained certification with the Association for Professional Chaplains. He is ordained in the independent Catholic movement, originally through the American Catholic Church (established 1915), and his lineage there includes ordination with the Philippine Independent Church which is in full communion with the Episcopal Church. He is a fully ordained Priest in the Ecumenical Catholic Church which is the only independent Catholic group to be a member of the National Council of Churches.

Tim is by training and by passion, a chaplain, a psychologist, an astrophysicist, a computer scientist, an author, and a musician (blues guitar and Middle Eastern oud). He currently serves as the staff chaplain at a hospice in the Los Angeles area of Southern California. He is an author of books on various topics from how to design and code computer games, to dealing with Alzheimer's, to coping with vision loss, to seminal work on Autism, as well as books on Zen, Christian meditation and other spiritual topics. He has also written a fantasy novel in the style of Douglas Adams and intends to write more fiction.

He is married to his wife Cheri, an English Professor, has two children, several grandchildren, two cats and a parrot. He and his wife live in Pasadena, California.

www.timlangdell.com
www.stillcenter.org
www.christbuddha.org
www.christwaybuddhaway.com
www.oxbridgepublications.com
and Tim's non-profit, www.kids-rights.org

Notes

<u>Notes</u>

<u>Notes</u>

<u>Notes</u>

Notes

<u>Notes</u>

www.ingramcontent.com/pod-product-compliance
Lightning Source LLC
Chambersburg PA
CBHW071610040426
42452CB00008B/1300